L.E.E.D.!

Listen, Engage, Empower & Drive Change

Copyright

This publication is intended for guidance purposes only and does not replace professional advice. References are provided to support learning, planning, and implementation. Inclusion does not imply endorsement, and readers should consult professionals for organization-specific legal, financial, or operational decisions.

Portions of this book were edited for grammar and clarity using OpenAI's GPT-5.2 model. Program templates included in this book were initially developed with the assistance of OpenAI's GPT-5.2 model and subsequently refined through substantial human review and editing.

© 2026 Joy Semien. All rights reserved.

Cover Photography by Shots by Beck

Cover Design by Lynette Ward, Netbooks LLC

No part of this book may be reproduced, distributed, or transmitted in any form or by any means, including photocopying, recording, or other electronic or mechanical methods, without the prior written permission of the author, except in the case of brief quotations embodied in critical reviews and certain other non-commercial uses permitted by copyright law. The views and opinions expressed in this book are those of the author and do not necessarily reflect the official policy or position of any organization, agency, or institution.

ISBN: 979-8-218-91494-3

L.E.E.D. With Joy

A Guide to Listening, Engaging, Empowering, and Driving Change

Joy Semien, Ph.D.

Table of Contents

Copyright 2

Letter From the Author

.... 7

Chapter 1. My Story, My Why, My Brand

My Story 9

Chapter 2. The L.E.E.D. With Joy Method 16

Chapter 3. Listening First: Where Lived Experience Meets Data 28

Chapter 4. Engagement: Moving From Hearing to Doing 41

Chapter 5. Empowerment through Education. 51

Chapter 6. Drive Change 59

Chapter 7: Lessons Learned & The L.E.E.D. With Joy Toolkit 88

   The Diary of A Program Manager: Lessons Learned 90

   The L.E.E.D. With Joy Toolkit 101

      Guide: Supporting Community-Based Organizations in Starting Their Own Business or Nonprofit 102

      Community Listening Checklist 106

      Key Stakeholder Map 108

      Stakeholder Letters 109

One-on-One Conversation Toolkit: Listening with Intent 115

Methods to Conduct Listening Sessions 117

      Sample Operational Agreements 127

      Sample Memorandum of Understanding (MOU) 131

Sample Scope of Work (SOW) – Detailed Template 135

      Sample Non-Disclosure Agreement (NDA) 139

      Sample Copyright Release Form 141

Data Sharing Agreement	143
Step-by-Step Guide to Running a Program or Workshop	145
Writing a Mission and a Vision Statement	149
Writing Program and Learning Objectives Using Bloom's Taxonomy	151
Introductory Meeting for Co-Creating a Program	155
Planning Document Overview	157
Program Planning Document	158
Sample Planning Meeting Agenda	160
Sample Task Timeline	161
Sample Assignment Timeline	162
Vendor Vetting Checklist	163
Vendor List	166
Logistics Contractor One-Pager	167
Logistics Contractor Training	172
Example Independent Contractor Agreement	176
Sample Training Protocols	181
Sample Invoice	186
Sample Order Form	187
Marketing Guidelines for Programs, Workshops, and Initiatives	188
Branding Guide	190
Guide for Holding a Planning Meeting With a CBO	193

Sample Sign-In Sheets 198

Run of Show Template 199

Community Program Budget Template 201

Program Impact and Success Measures 202

Sample Partner Feedback Form 206

References 209

About the Author 212

Other Books By Joy Semien 214

About L.E.E.D. With Joy LLC 215

Letter From the Author

Dear L.E.E.D.er,

Do you remember being in school and receiving that essay question: "What do you want to be or do when you grow up?" It was almost always followed by, "What is your definition of success?"

My answers to the first question were never consistent. Some days I wrote that I wanted to be a teacher, an architect, a writer, or even a marine biologist. Ironically, over the years, I have worked in all these fields.

But my answer to the second question never wavered. I would always write, "I will be successful if I can put a smile on one person's face every day." I am not sure why that answer never changed, but here I am, years later, and it remains the foundation for everything I do.

What began as an essay response eventually became my brand—all rooted in the simple desire to put a smile on someone's face each day. This definition of success has guided every decision I have made, personally and professionally. It shapes how I show up in rooms, how I serve others, and how I approach my work. Long before L.E.E.D. With Joy became a business, it was simply the way I chose to live.

This book is both a reflection and a roadmap. It tells the story of how L.E.E.D. With Joy came to be, what it stands for, and how purpose-driven education can transform communities when designed with intention and led with joy.

I hope that as you read this book, you will gain practical insights that allow you to L.E.E.D. With Joy in your own life and career. The book introduces the principles, phases, and accountability measures of the L.E.E.D. With Joy Method.

This book is organized into two major sections. The first, The L.E.E.D. With Joy Method, introduces the framework that guides my approach to community work, emphasizing research, engagement, and co-creation to drive meaningful impact. The second section, The Toolkit, provides practical strategies, exercises, and resources that readers can apply in their own work, offering hands-on guidance to complement the principles presented in the first section.

While the principles in this book are not new, the way they are framed is unique. For scholars who read this text, you will notice it is not heavily burdened with research or citations, as my goal was to make it accessible to readers who are not academics. References are included at the back of the book for those who wish to explore further, but ultimately, this book focuses on the lessons I have learned through my own work and how they can support others pursuing similar paths.

This book is for those ready to move beyond surface-level engagement and toward work that builds trust, strengthens capacity, and leaves communities stronger long after a project ends.

With joy and purpose,

Dr. Joy Semien

Chapter 1. My Story, My Why, My Brand

My Story

Over the last few years, I've found myself asking, "Who am I?" and "Who do I want to be?" Questions like that make you stop and really think about your story.

You see, I was born in Houston, Texas, but I didn't grow up there. I grew up in a small town called Geismar, Louisiana, a fenceline community tucked along the Mississippi River. Many of the families there (like mine) were descendants of slaves, carrying generations of history, strength, and survival.

This history shaped the rhythm of the community, the way people worked, laughed, fought for justice, and leaned on one another. Growing up there, you could feel both the weight of the past and the stubborn, joyful spirit that kept everyone moving forward.

All of that history and strength existed alongside the harsh reality of daily life, where the community's resilience was tested every time the air carried the smells and dangers of the nearby industrial plants.

Open a window or a door, and you'd get a big whiff of what the old folks called the "good ole smell of money." That was life in the heart of Cancer Alley. Geismar is tiny—just a ten-mile radius, but it's home to over 15 industrial facilities.

Most days growing up, my sister and I played on our outdoor swing sets and tire swing, with our grandmother pushing us, or running between our great aunts' and uncles' homes collecting frozen cups, cinnamon cakes, and, of course, the family gossip.

But some days were different, sirens would go off, and we'd have to run inside because one of the plants had released sulfuric acid into the air, a deadly toxin that can cause chemical burns, blindness, and other serious health problems when overly exposed.

We would experience days when the air was so toxic it sent my sister and me to the hospital for breathing treatments and sent my family to local law offices trying to get justice for the exposure.

That "good ole smell of money" that everyone joked about was making money for some, but for so many of the people living next door, it eventually brought cancer and other health problems from constant exposure to what these facilities were putting into the air.

Sometimes I reflect on those days and remember sitting in community meetings with my grandmother and my mom, listening to the arguments about what to do next.

I remember some people were in favor of the plants, while others wanted justice—or at least a little money to help cover new health expenses linked to the exposure.

I remember relatives fighting to prevent massive chemical trucks from passing in front of our homes. I remember rust-colored cars, doors, and windows. But what I remember most of all is that, after all the fighting and arguments, the community came together with joy and shared food.

They didn't always agree, and they didn't always get it right, but the joy that kept them together—surrounded by family and friends—is what made them keep going. I believe this is where I first learned to *L.E.E.D. With Joy*.

You see, the community members living in Geismar all had a shared agenda of wanting a better life for their families, friends, and loved ones.

> *However, they also knew it wasn't going to happen overnight, so while they fought for justice and change, they also built a sense of community and love grounded in joy!*

Unfortunately, many people from this community passed away without seeing the fruits of their labor. They died from cancer and other diseases that some scientists believe were linked to ongoing exposure to chemical pollutants. They died while being ignored by politicians and government officials who denied there was any wrongdoing.

They died without seeing the full change they had fought so hard to achieve. But because they pursued justice, I can walk through doors my ancestors could only dream of, and I can be the change agent they so desperately needed. I carry their stories with me wherever I go—they serve as the foundation for *My Why*.

My Why

I was once asked, "What is my Why?" and until that moment, I had never really thought about it. But over time, I came to realize that "My Why" is deeply tied to where I grew up. You see, in my community, risk was normalized, environmental exposure was normalized, resources were limited, and residents faced systemic neglect.

Long before I had the language for environmental justice, disaster resilience, or community capacity building, I understood what it meant to live at the intersection of vulnerability and survival.

By the time I turned 13 and my mom bought a computer for my sister and me, the first thing I did was look up the EPA—the Environmental Protection Agency.

I wanted to know what pollutants we were exposed to, the legal limits for what facilities could release into the Mississippi River—the very place where we fished to supplement food when our family could not afford groceries—and how much they were allowed to release into the air we breathed while playing outside on the swings with our grandmother and her siblings.

My Why is tied to those lived experiences. It is tied to the climate deniers, the government officials who bow to industrial facilities to secure a dollar for their own families while leaving others behind.

What is my Why?

My Why is simple: community members deserve clean air, water, and soil, so they don't have to watch their loved ones die from preventable pollution or disasters (natural or manmade).

My Why is the ability to provide local nonprofits, grassroots agencies, and everyday people with the tools they need to live healthy, joyful lives without the fear of dying from environmental harm.

Contrary to popular belief, our realities were not abstract; they were real, lived experiences shared by the entire community.

Don't mind me if I go on a bit of a rant here...but what fires me up more than anything is hearing people deny that these realities exist. And it's not just along the Mississippi River corridor where I grew up; this is happening across the United States.

Pollutants are poisoning Indigenous lands, and Native Americans are dying of cancer from excessive radiation exposure. People in the Appalachians cannot access clean water because there is limited quality infrastructure. In Alaska, whales are dying, and Indigenous communities are going without their traditional resources.

And the problem doesn't stop in the United States...it's global!

Whole islands are being flooded and destroyed by hurricanes, tsunamis, typhoons, and floods. Countries like Mexico and South America have serious infrastructure problems that often lead to problems right here in the United States.

All their stories matter. Yet the people we elect to protect us often deny any connection between our actions and these lived experiences. They dismiss our realities, turning them into abstract, nonexistent ideas.

Well, I'm here to tell you—these realities are real. They exist. And more companies, academics, community leaders, and officials need to stand up for those who cannot stand up for themselves.

That's exactly why I created L.E.E.D. With Joy.

My Brand

My brand is grounded in this idea of education as a pathway to understanding the failure of systems; not just how they work, but who they work for and who they leave behind. As I moved through formal training in science, planning, and policy, collecting degrees and certifications that most people would ever desire. I realized that knowledge alone does not create change.

Remember this: you could be the smartest person in the room, with the most detailed information and complex graphics, but if that information is not translated so that others in the room can access it, then it's still inaccessible.

You can have all the data in the world, but if that data isn't linked to the lived experience of communities, then it will never go over well, and solutions designed without community input often fail the people they are meant to support.

The reason why I started this chapter with my story is that my story is inseparable from the brand because authenticity is not a marketing strategy; it is a standard.

Every curriculum, training, and program developed under L.E.E.D. With Joy reflects a commitment to meeting people where they are while refusing to lower expectations for what they can achieve.

I believe communities already possess knowledge, resilience, and creativity; what is often missing are tools, resources, and systems that recognize and invest in those strengths.

At the core of my brand is the belief that we should enter communities by first listening to what they have to say. Through engagement and empowerment, we can then drive meaningful change. Programs and projects should be culturally responsive and actionable, while also cultivating Joy. So I built a brand to reflect just that.

Reflect on Your Why...
Why Do You Do This Work?

What Type of Leader Are You?

Chapter 2. The L.E.E.D. With Joy Method

Community work often fails not because of a lack of funding, data, or good intentions, but because of a disconnect between systems and the people they are designed to serve.

Too frequently, programs are built for communities rather than with them, relying on larger nonprofits, short-term engagement, rigid metrics, and practices that prioritize reporting over relationships.

I designed the L.E.E.D. With the Joy framework as a response to these gaps and the need to translate research into actionable programs. The L.E.E.D. With Joy Method centers community knowledge as expertise, relationships as infrastructure, and education as a tool for shared power.

It provides a structured yet flexible approach for practitioners, organizations, and institutions seeking to do community work that is ethical, effective, and sustainable.

It emerged from my lived experience, combined with years of working across education, disaster preparedness, environmental justice, and organizational capacity building, where I observed the same pattern repeated across sectors; communities were expected to adapt to systems that were never designed with their realities in mind.

The Framework

To L.E.E.D. means to **listen** first, to **engage**, to **empower,** and to **drive** change. This framework is not theoretical; it is data-grounded, practice-informed, and community-driven.

At its core, the method recognizes a simple truth: sustainable change does not happen without people. Too often, both good and bad decisions are made for communities without their voices and their presence at the table.

Time and time again, I have seen funders pursue projects in communities without first listening to residents, only to be surprised when those efforts fail.

This is not a new phenomenon; scholars like Enenkel et. al. (2017), Gundlach and McDonogh (2011), and Nance (2009) have repeatedly pointed out that moving from a top-down method does not work, but moving with the community as a key stakeholder does work!

The L.E.E.D. With Joy Method disrupts that pattern by centering listening as the first and most critical step.

Listening, in this context, is not passive or performative; it is intentional, ongoing, and rooted in respect for lived experience.

It requires slowing down, creating and/or being in the right spaces, asking the right questions, and being willing to hear and address answers that may challenge assumptions or timelines.

Listen

By prioritizing listening from the beginning, the method shifts power back to the community. It ensures that decisions are informed by those most affected and that solutions are grounded in real needs rather than external agendas.

Listening sets the foundation for trust, accountability, and long-term impact, making every step that follows more effective and sustainable.

Let's look at a case study where <u>Listening</u> was a critical first step in the development of a program. A few years back, I had an amazing opportunity to work with a funder who wanted to sponsor programming in a local community. The funder had their goals, metrics, and objectives.

They knew what they wanted to do and how they wanted the program designed. They had completed footwork to gauge community interest and even obtain potential topics. They did this through focus groups and interviews. Prior to my involvement in the project.

By the time I was invited to support the project, the hard qualitative and quantitative data were compiled and ready to go. In this instance, the stakeholders had done the initial footwork of inviting the broader community to share their opinions on what they wanted to see in their own communities.

The difficulty was not a lack of community input, but a failure to center it. Despite community members clearly voicing their needs, implementation decisions were driven by stakeholder agendas rather than community priorities.

Here is the thing its not enough just to listen. In the L.E.E.D. With Joy framework, the first step is to listen with the intent to hear and act. Not just checking off a box.

When we seek to listen actively, we can ensure that not only are voices heard, but they also have a seat at the planning table.

I was deeply involved in the implementation of the program, but to be completely honest, in hindsight, there were critical steps that were missed!

While their was multiple problems with this design, one of the biggest problems was that the community was not a continuous key stakeholder; these programs and initiatives were designed for them and not by them. In hindsight, we should have returned to the community to confirm that they were aware of the program and to ensure the final programming was still aligned with their interests and priorities.

The reality: My team and I did all the work, designed the program, and guess what, only four people came out to an event that was designed for 30! I was devastated, the funder was upset, and all of the people we had secured as speakers and vendors were disappointed because of the low turnout.

Lesson Learned: The biggest lesson I learned here is that listening is not a one-time action; it's continuous, and I did not <u>revisit the community and listen again.</u> This amazing program came to an abrupt halt as we reassessed how we should move forward.

Engagement:

The next step in the model is <u>engagement</u>. Engagement at its core is a step-pass listening because it seeks to actively involve the community as stakeholders, partners, and co-creators. It creates opportunity for intentionality, consistency, and trust building.

It ensures that the community is an active participant with a strong relationship built over time, rather than just one-and-done. When engagement is done well, it builds shared ownership and accountability.

Community members are not just participants; they become collaborators who help guide the direction of projects and programs. This is where trust deepens, and the foundation for long-term change begins to take shape.

Let's revisit the case study I mentioned above. Another major component that was missing from the implementation phase was that it was not built <u>with</u> the community, but rather <u>for</u> the community.

When we revisited our implementation strategy, it became clear that the missing element was positioning the community as the lead stakeholder. When the community leads, their voices guide decision-making, their ideas shape implementation, and they move from participants to co-creators. This shared ownership fosters collective responsibility and builds trust that is essential for lasting impact.

> *When we redesigned the program, we centered on the community in every decision.*

Community-based organizations were engaged as co-creators, not recipients. Together, we co-designed the program structure, selected supplies, identified relevant topics, curated giveaways, developed marketing strategies, and chose speakers.

Our role shifted from directing the process to facilitating it, which was the critical element missing from the original approach. We also empowered them to select the locations where the events would be held, making the spaces more accessible, familiar, and welcoming for community members.

When we co-created with the community, we had higher attendance numbers, we had stronger engagement, and community members showed genuine interest in supporting the work.

Empower

The next step in the model is <u>empowerment</u>. Empowerment moves beyond participation and focuses on building capacity, confidence, and ownership within the community. It ensures that community members and organizations are not just involved in the process, but equipped with the knowledge, tools, and resources needed to sustain the work long after a program or project ends.

Through empowerment, communities gain the ability to make informed decisions, advocate for themselves, and lead initiatives that reflect their priorities, just like in the case study above.

This step shifts power from external actors to local leaders and institutions, reinforcing self-determination and long-term resilience. Empowerment is where engagement turns into action, and where communities begin to see themselves not as recipients of support, but as drivers of change.

Let's go back to the case study so I can show you why this step is so important. We listened to the community and started co-creating programs with them, for their community members. But here's the hard truth: many of the community leaders we worked with didn't have the resources, the tools, the time, or sometimes even the knowledge to pull these events off on their own.

Instead of dismissing them for what they didn't have, we lifted them up. We provided one-on-one training, created toolkits, guidebooks, and practical resources that made it possible for them to run the programs successfully.

We met them where they were, gave them what they needed, and turned their ideas into action. That's what empowerment really looks like. In fact, many of those guides and resources can be found throughout this book as helpful resources for you.

Drive

The next step in the model is <u>Drive</u>. This is where our entire model comes together. In everything we do, we aim to drive real, lasting change that is measurable, equitable, and community informed. It's not just about ideas, plans, or programs—it's about taking action that improves lives, strengthens communities, and ensures that the work we do today has an impact that lasts well into tomorrow.

My goal is that this impact lasts long after my team and I are gone—beyond our involvement, beyond the funders, and beyond any single stakeholder. True change sticks when communities have the tools, knowledge, and ownership to keep moving forward on their own.

In the case study, my team and I were intentional in our effort to train community members with the tools they needed to be successful. We ensured that we had shared learning experiences, provided training, toolkits, and resources that they could access even after the duration of the program.

The final step in the framework is to L.E.E.D. with Joy!

Joy is the pivotal component of this entire model. What distinguishes the L.E.E.D. With Joy Method is the intentional inclusion of joy. Joy is not treated as an afterthought or a soft outcome. It is a strategy.

Joy sustains people through difficult conversations, long processes, and systemic resistance. It is what allows communities to remain engaged, hopeful, and resilient even when the work is hard.

Take our case study, for example. The one thing that sustained all of us throughout the program was the joy exuded by the community members who attended each workshop. Regardless of the challenges we faced, the smiles, laughter, and energy in every room were the integral components that kept us motivated to keep implementing programs.

When people truly enjoy what they do, the work feels less like work and more like a fun activity. But when there is no joy—when there is strife, confusion, or division, the work becomes exhausting, draining, and almost impossible to sustain.

In my work, I have seen firsthand the absence of joy and the toll it can take on workplaces again and again. It's sad to witness so many people go without joy.

Sadly, joy is often misunderstood in professional and leadership spaces. It is frequently framed as optional, personal, or secondary to urgency, particularly in fields that address crisis, inequity, and harm.

The absence of joy is not a sign of seriousness; it is often a symptom of burnout-driven leadership and extractive systems. Joy is not the opposite of rigor; it is a prerequisite for sustainability.

In community work, leadership that is rooted solely in urgency and deficit narratives inevitably exhausts both practitioners and participants.

When leaders operate without joy, decision-making becomes reactive, relationships become transactional, and long-term vision is replaced by short-term survival. Not to mention, people just hate to come to work.

Joy, as a leadership imperative, functions as both a stabilizing force and a strategic tool. Leaders who center joy are better equipped to build trust, navigate conflict, and remain accountable to the communities they serve without sacrificing their own well-being or that of their teams.

I saw this firsthand in my role as Chief of Staff. When I first started, I honestly had no clue what I had gotten myself into. Everything was so structured—so many written and unwritten rules to follow. Meetings seemed endless, with little to no enjoyable moments.

On one hand, the role I played was serious. It affected a lot of people and could not be taken lightly. But on the other hand, the staff was burned out, exhausted from constant challenges, and drained. Some days, I dreaded going to work—until I remembered my answer to that essay question I shared at the beginning of this book: I would be successful if I could put a smile on at least one person's face every day. That became my personal mission.

I started small. I walked into meetings early, greeting people like "Bugs Bunny" with a cheerful:

"What's up, y'all?"

I approached colleagues in the hallways with smiles, jokes, and small stories. I sent ridiculous memes, shared silly anecdotes—all to make someone smile. And you know what happened? People started smiling. Meetings became lighter. Staff enjoyed coming in and interacting with each other.

In my role, we traveled a lot around the region for community meetings. Initially, the routine was exhausting: arrive at the event, return to the hotel, and catch a plane the next day—no balance, no fun. I made a simple rule: after 5:00, work stops, and everyone traveling with us must do one fun thing, no matter what it is.

What I realized was powerful: when we intentionally introduced a little joy and a little fun, people's lives changed. They loved coming with us. The work became enjoyable, not overwhelming. They laughed more, smiled more, and approached the people we were sent to help differently.

I only spent a few months in this position, but in that short time, a shift occurred. And it all came down to a little joy, a little intention, and remembering why we do the work in the first place.

The L.E.E.D. With Joy Method can be applied across sectors: education, nonprofit work, government, business, and grassroots organizing. Whether working with students, residents, organizations, or agencies, the method provides a clear, adaptable framework for building trust, increasing agency, and turning lived experience into action.

It is important to note that these steps are not linear checkboxes; they are interconnected practices that build trust, strengthen capacity, and move communities from participation to ownership.

This is not a one-size-fits-all solution. It is a responsive method designed to meet communities where they are while supporting them in getting where they want to go, together.

In the remaining chapters, I will break each one of these steps further, providing strategies and resources that can help you in your journey to L.E.E.D. With Joy!

How do You L.E.E.D.

What's a Leadership Quality You Admire Most?

Chapter 3. Listening First: Where Lived Experience Meets Data

As someone who spent many years in school and ultimately earned a PhD, I can tell you the question I heard most often was,

- Where is the data?
- Is your work grounded in data?
- What does literature say?

To be honest, I hated that part. Numbers were never really my thing. Very few scholars valued qualitative data like interviews or lived experiences, so while I knew data mattered, I often found it boring, confusing, and at times deeply frustrating.

My professors would constantly remind me: The answer is in the data. Without data, you cannot prove the problem exists.

That drove me crazy.

But here is the truth: they were not wrong. Data is important. It does tell a story, and it is necessary. But it is not everything. Data is only one piece of the story.

To understand the full picture, you have to talk to the people the data describes. You have to go into the field. You must listen to their pain, their frustrations, and see their lived realities. You must witness firsthand what those numbers represent.

Data without lived experience is just numbers on a page or words in a report. But when you combine data with lived experience, the story becomes visible in a way numbers alone never could.

One of the clearest examples of this approach is the work of Jacob Riis, a Danish immigrant, journalist, and social reformer. Riis picked up a camera and documented tenement housing conditions in New York City.

He published his photographs in a book called "How the Other Half Lives." He used imagery to expose the depth of poverty and unsafe living conditions that statistics alone had failed to move people to address.

> *Sometimes, numbers are not enough to create change. Sometimes change requires listening; truly listening; and using those stories as the foundation for action.*

Listening with the Intent to Act

For most people, listening is hard. We do not always listen with the true intention to hear and act. More often than not, we listen with the intention to respond. I know this firsthand. It is one of my biggest flaws and, honestly, the thing that has gotten me into the most trouble over the years; not truly listening.

I remember being a child and my parents asking me to do something. Because I was distracted or already thinking ahead, I would only do part of what they asked. Not because I was disobedient, but because I only heard part of the instruction.

As an adult, now running multiple organizations, that habit could easily become a liability. My mind moves fast; sometimes a hundred miles a minute, and if I am not intentional, I can miss important details or forget what was said altogether. And if I am not careful, I can even find myself talking over someone who is taking the time to fully share their thoughts.

That is why I now make it a point to slow down, give my full attention, and keep a pen and paper nearby. Writing things down forces me to stay present and accountable.

Here are some steps I have put into place in recent years to ensure that I am listening with the intent of hearing and acting:

- If I am in a virtual meeting, I keep my mic on mute. I write down my thoughts and use the hand raise feature, waiting for the facilitator to call on me before speaking.
- If I am in an in-person meeting, I often sit with one hand over my mouth and the other holding a pen, writing down my thoughts so I do not interrupt.
- Before responding to someone's comments, I reflect on what I heard to make sure I fully understand and to avoid making assumptions.
- I do my best to close the loop by communicating next steps so that listening is not passive, but a catalyst for moving forward.
- I have learned to use phrases like: "
- "What I'm hearing you say is…"
- "Let me make sure I understand this correctly…"
- "Can you help me understand this a bit more?"
- "When you say ___, what does that look like in practice?"
- "Am I capturing this accurately?"
- "I understand your point"
- "Let's pause for a moment."
- "Before we move on, I want to acknowledge what was just said."
- "I'd love to hear from someone we haven't heard from."
- "That's helpful feedback; thank you."
- "I hadn't considered it that way before."

- "I need to sit with that for a moment."
- "I can see how our approach may have missed the mark."
- "Here's what I'm committing to based on what I heard."
- "Based on the conversation, our next step will be…"
- "Who should lead this, and what support is needed?"
- "By when we should follow up?"
- "We're in this together."
- "Thank you for trusting us with this."
- "This work is hard, but it matters."
- "Let's take a breath and keep going."

I had to teach myself how to listen to hear, not just to acknowledge, and to be willing to act on what was shared. Because listening without action is just noise.

I had to learn this the hard way, you see, I'm a person that doesn't naturally like confrontation. In fact, I will run from it if I can. But when you own multiple businesses, and you are juggling multiple personalities from employees, funders, and clients, sometimes you just have to pull your big girl pants up and start communicating with purpose.

I remember in my role as chief of staff, there was a heated conversation between an employee and a supervisor. The level of disrespect the employee displayed was alarming, and in that moment, I knew I had to intervene quickly. I did so use simple, intentional communication. I remember saying, "I understand your point, and we will take it under consideration. For now, let's focus on how we move our current task forward." That single shift in language helped de-escalate the situation, bring the conversation back to purpose, and allowed us to end the call productively.

You see, sometimes L.E.E.D.ing with Joy is simply about making sure a passionate employee feels heard and validated. We are all human—we have good days and bad days—and sometimes we just need a little support to get through them. Proper communication can lead to de-escalation and create space for collaboration, understanding, and productive problem-solving. When people feel heard and respected, even tense situations can turn into opportunities for connection and progress.

Understanding Community Ecosystems

Once we've mastered intentional listening and clear communication, the next step is understanding the community itself—the ecosystem in which people live, work, and play.

Communities are more than a collection of individuals; they are living systems shaped by history, culture, resources, and the challenges they face. To make meaningful changes, we must see the whole picture, not just isolated problems.

Before bringing programs and initiatives into a community, it is important that we understand the entire community ecosystem, ensuring as many community voices are heard and implemented in every part of the process.

The integration of community voices is the foundation for implementing an effective community program and initiative. This is called a place-based approach.

A place-based approach taps into a community's past and present to determine its future trajectory! Its about meeting people where they are, understanding their uniqueness, and tailoring programs, resources, and information to fit the community.

In using a place-based approach, we move away from a top-down, one-size-fits-all model to a strategy designed to resonate with all people and places that will have a lasting impact.

Place-based approaches are intentional… this approach requires the facilitator to ask key questions like:

1. Who in the community should be involved in co-creating this program?
2. Who is the program designed for?
3. Who will be impacted by the program?
4. Who are we leaving out?
5. Why are we doing this program?
6. How will we reach people?
7. How do community members prefer to communicate and receive information?
8. What incentives or supports do people need to fully participate?
9. How many people will the program reach?
10. Are we creating a space for the whole family or just a portion of the family?
11. Who will benefit the most, and who will lose the most?
12. Are there groups that are often left out, and how can we include them?
13. What issues matter most to the community right now?
14. What solutions have been tried before, and what worked or didn't work?
15. What resources (time, money, knowledge, space) are available locally?
16. How does the community define success for this initiative?

17. How will we know the program is making a meaningful difference?

18. What metrics or outcomes matter most to the community?

Using a place-based strategy is not a new concept; it is a concept that many scholars, corporations, and government officials sometimes forget to integrate into their programs and initiatives.

In using a place-based approach, we can tap into the knowledge of members of the community and the leaders who work diligently to provide resources to those in need. If we ask the right questions and take the time to listen. Check out chapter 7 for a full list of questions to ask before stepping into a community.

Tools to Use a Place-based Approach

A major step in implementing a place-based approach is to know the community you are planning to work in. This can be done by performing a simple assessment called "A Community Profile."

A Community Profile is a tool that allows us to assess community assets like cultural/religious facilities, hospitals, schools, parks, homes, businesses, religious facilities, and nonprofit organizations; to speak to the localized grass-roots community-based organizations who are on the ground doing the work in these same communities; to identify challenges and needs of the localized communities. These are the voices that are integral to ensuring a place-based approach.

A community profile is simply a written description of a community that outlines every possible component of the community you would like to work in. A community profile most commonly consists of the following sections:

- Community Overview
- Demographic Profile

- Social and Cultural Characteristics
- Health and Wellbeing Indicators
- Economic Conditions
- Environmental and Physical Conditions
- Community Assets and Resources
- Community Needs and Challenges
- Governance and Political Landscape
- Stakeholders and Partnership Landscape
- Existing Programs and Services
- Risk and Vulnerability Assessment

Each component of the community profile seeks to give an overview of the community to provide a visual depiction of the challenges and strengths of the community.

Many groups often skip this step, but let me explain why it's so important. A while back, I had a client ask me to develop a set of programs on their behalf. The client was very specific — they wanted it done at a particular location, at a particular time, and around very specific topics in a very large city.

This created a BIG problem. The people they wanted to reach were not in those locations, and they were not willing to be bused there.

As a result, the entire program had low attendance. Even though I tried hard to explain that this large city was heavily segregated, the client insisted on conducting the program their way.

When we reassessed how to get more people to participate, I took the client on a tour of the city. I showed them the divisiveness of the neighborhoods, explained the history, pointed out areas of heavy pollution, and highlighted systemic racism. I used all of my knowledge of this community to demonstrate how their vision did not align with the realities on the ground.

We regrouped and began talking to stakeholders about what would actually work. Eventually, we settled on a new model, using locations directly in the communities they wished to serve. And guess what? Turnout improved, people were more receptive, and the client was happy.

Moral of the story: **DON'T SKIP THIS STEP!**

The next step is to conduct a *stakeholder map*. A stakeholder map is a toolkit that identifies key stakeholders in the community who can be an asset to the initiative or program you are designing. This list should consist of individuals, organizations, government officials, religious leaders, or other prominent officials in the community. The table below outlines some of the information that you can collect when identifying a key stakeholder.

Stakeholder Type	Organization Name	Point of Contact Name	Phone #	E-mail	Address

Once you have a list of stakeholders its important to start entering them into a Customer Relationship Management (CRM) database. These can be companies like Brevo, Mailchimp, and Constant Contact, Hubspot, Monday.com, Go High Level. There are many out there to choose from. Do your research and use the one that best fits your needs and budget.

Alternatively, you can do this in excel creating tabs and filters. Then copy the e-mail addresses into your e-mail software and begin e-mailing ideal stakeholders to get them involved in the work that you are doing. (See Chapter 7 for some example letters you can use to contact key stakeholders).

After gathering and contacting your list of stakeholders, it's important that you then bring them together and/or schedule meetings to discuss with each party your goals, missions, objectives, and acquire feedback on the implementation of the proposed community initiative. Here are some methods you can use to create listening sessions with your key stakeholders:

Methods to Conduct Listening Sessions

- **Interviews:** One-on-one conversations with stakeholders to hear their perspectives, experiences, and priorities. This allows for deep understanding and individualized attention.
- **Focus Groups:** Small group discussions that encourage dialogue among stakeholders. Focus groups can reveal common themes, differences of opinion, and collective priorities.
- **Community Surveys:** Written or digital surveys distributed to a broader audience. They help capture quantitative and qualitative data from a large group of stakeholders efficiently.

- **Town Hall Meetings:** Open meetings where stakeholders can share thoughts publicly. These forums promote transparency, build trust, and allow the community to hear each other's perspectives.
- **Observation/Field Visits:** Spending time in the community or organization to observe how people interact, use resources, and experience their environment. This helps to uncover needs that may not be voiced directly.
- **Workshops or Co-Creation Sessions:** Interactive sessions where stakeholders actively participate in designing solutions or programs. This ensures their ideas and priorities shape the initiative from the start.
- **Storytelling Sessions:** Providing a space for stakeholders to share personal experiences or narratives. Stories provide context, emotion, and insight that data alone cannot capture.
- **Listening Tours:** Structured visits to multiple sites or groups within a community to hear a variety of perspectives. This helps ensure diverse voices are included in decision-making.
- **Advisory Committees or Councils:** A group of key stakeholders who meet regularly to provide guidance, feedback, and recommendations throughout the program lifecycle.
- **Digital Platforms/Forums:** Online spaces where stakeholders can comment, share ideas, or ask questions. It is useful for reaching participants who may not attend in-person sessions.
- **Conversation:** One-on-one discussions with a stakeholder to hear their perspective, experiences, and priorities. This method allows for deep understanding and builds trust while uncovering insights that may not emerge in group settings.

These are just a few strategies that we use when L.E.E.D.ing with Joy. While none of these strategies are new and are all grounded in the historical strategies of those who came before us, they are tools we regularly use to guide us as we learn to listen intently and act accordingly. (See chapter 7 for one-pagers that can help you implement each type of listening session).

Describe Your Ideal Community Based Partnership

Chapter 4. Engagement: Moving From Hearing to Doing

Engagement, in my framework, is more than listening — it's actively involving the community as partners, co-creators, and decision-makers. It's collaborating with purpose and making sure those most affected are also most heard.

I can't tell you how many times I've seen projects and initiatives fail – not because the projects themselves were designed poorly or the intentions were bad – but simply because people weren't aware of the program, they were not actively involved, and they were not key stakeholders.

You see, engagement is about co-creation, having real partners who help to guide the initiative.

> *The truth is, without real community buy-in its almost impossible for programs and initiatives to really flourish.*

I learned this lesson the hard way while working on my master's thesis. I had this great idea: I would go home to my small town of Geismar, Louisiana, and teach the people I grew up with "How to Be Prepared for Disasters."

I just knew it would work. I had the curriculum, I had food, I had free disaster kits — but when I hosted the first workshop, only two people showed up.

It didn't take long to figure out why. I had no big community stakeholders supporting me, nobody really knew me, and I used to be painfully shy. I had a heart for people, but the boldness of a mouse.

If I wanted to graduate and move forward with my life, I had to break out of my shell. I had to go meet people, stop hiding behind my mom like I so often did, and find key stakeholders who could help recruit community members to attend.

It took a few months and several workshops later, but eventually I had recruited 30 people to attend these events—and that's when I realized the real power of engagement.

That experience taught me something I've carried ever since: real engagement takes more than ideas and resources—it takes trust, presence, and relationships. Without them, even the best plan will fail.

Defining Engagement: What is it and why does it matter?

According to the International Association for Public Participation, engagement "is the process of actively involving individuals or communities in decision-making, planning, and implementation, ensuring their voices, perspectives, and needs shape outcomes." Essentially, it means asking people to play a key role in the implementation process.

So, let's break down what it means to engage with a community and its stakeholders effectively. In our model, engagement is all about co-creating through collaboration because meaningful change does not happen when decisions are made in isolation.

Engagement moves beyond informing communities or asking for input after plans are already set. Instead, it invites community members, organizations, and stakeholders into the process as equal partners from the very beginning.

Co-creating through collaboration means programs, initiatives, and workshops are developed together, priorities are identified collectively, and the curation process reflects both lived experience and technical expertise.

The community is not treated as a recipient of services, but as a driver of the work. This approach builds shared ownership, strengthens trust, and increases the likelihood that programs will be relevant, accessible, and sustainable.

When collaboration is genuine, engagement becomes a two-way exchange. Communities contribute their knowledge of place, culture, and need, while partners contribute resources, capacity, and support. Resulting in initiatives grounded in reality, responsive to community priorities, and capable of creating lasting impact.

Let's reflect on the case study I presented to you in Chapter 2. I had an opportunity to plan an initiative that at first was grounded in only what the funder wanted, and while the initiative began by asking the community what they wanted, they were not involved in the overall planning and development of the program.

When we reassessed and began to actively involve the community in the development process, we had better outcomes. It's not enough to just listen; you must seek to involve the community in every part of the process.

Remember this: you will not always get it right. Things will not always work. People will be people, and disagreements will arise. What matters most is the ability to pause, reassess, and move forward when needed.

Engagement: The Good, The Bad, and The Ugly

Let us be honest for a moment. Engagement is not easy. It takes time, patience, humility, and a willingness to give up control. I have watched engagement bring people together in powerful ways, and I have also seen it fall apart because of ego, misalignment, and poor communication. That is why it is important to talk openly about the good, the bad, and the ugly as it relates to engagement.

So, let's break down the good, the bad, and the ugly.

I will start with the "good." Ultimately, the benefit of engaging community-based stakeholders is that more people are brought to the table, more ideas are shared, bigger visions are cultivated, and, ideally, a diverse and meaningful program can be developed and implemented.

Engaging community-based stakeholders as co-creators can change the entire trajectory of a program or an initiative. When people who live, work, and play in a community are invited into the process early, trust begins to form. That trust is built on mutual respect, cultivated in lived experiences and local knowledge.

Communities know what works best in their neighbourhoods, they know what will and has failed, and they know the physical and social barriers that still exist. When their voices are intertwined in the programming, the programming becomes relevant, accessible, and by far more effective.

Strong engagement also encourages community involvement. Community leaders are often the gatekeepers; without their participation, community members often do not show up and actively participate. This is because when the community leader is active and present, the program feels like home – it's tangible, it's often safe, and relatable.

An important thing to remember is that every community is different – having someone invested in the community can help you navigate seen and unseen challenges. Strong collaborations can also reduce resistance from the community and reduce misunderstandings. By creating space for collaboration early on, concerns can be addressed before they become real problems.

Engagement through co-creation shifts the mindset from "your project" to "our project," building shared ownership and accountability.

In fact, people are often more willing to commit time, energy, and resources when they feel invested in the outcome.

A major benefit of co-creation is that over time, the process builds local capacity and leadership. Community-based organizations gain tools, confidence, and experience that extend beyond a single project. This strengthens sustainability, allowing initiatives to continue long after funding ends or external partners step away.

Most importantly, engagement elevates voices that are often overlooked, reaching residents who do not show up in surveys or public meetings. In doing so, it grounds the work in principles of equity and justice by ensuring those most impacted help shape the decisions that affect their lives. That's the "Good."

Now, let us talk about the *bad and the ugly*. In a perfect world, engagement would come with little to no challenges, and everyone would work together in harmony. Unfortunately, we do not live in a perfect world.

In my work, I cannot tell you how many times I have heard people say that engagement is unnecessary or too difficult. As a result, people rush past this step or reduce it to something they can simply check off a list.

I will admit that it can be challenging. It takes extra time to cultivate relationships, bring everyone together, sort through various ideals, and ensure you have the right stakeholders in place to help bring your vision to life. But its worth it!

Project coordinators don't always realize that it's the local grassroots, community-based organizations and nonprofits that hold the keys to the community.

These groups carry the voices and the stories of those who need help the most. I have seen it over and over—big funders refusing to support the "little people," instead giving large sums to big nonprofits because they have stronger operations, better impact measures, and larger visibility.

But here's the catch: those larger organizations also have higher overhead costs, and often they fail to reach the people who don't show up in surveys or at citywide community meetings.

Don't get me wrong—the big organizations need funding too, and they should receive it.

But the small mom-and-pop shops and local community-based organizations that give out of their own paychecks also deserve a shot at those big dollars.

It frustrates me so much sometimes. I see philanthropic organizations swoop into communities, pour money into programming, and within a year or two, leave just as fast as they came—redirecting resources from the local grassroots groups to these global nonprofits. And the communities? They're left behind.

Now, don't get me wrong, while there are many benefits to working with local groups, there are also many challenges. Engaging the community is not always an easy process, and that's the *ugly* part.

People have different priorities, limited time, and sometimes mistrust of outsiders or even well-meaning initiatives. Conflicting agendas can arise between stakeholders, and if you're not careful, the process can slow down or even stall entirely.

I've seen programs get stuck in endless meetings or bogged down by miscommunication—all because the right relationships weren't built from the start. I've also seen what happens when stakeholders bring in additional people who don't share the vision and are only looking out for themselves.

They don't listen, they're not team players, and their presence can derail the entire process. The key is to acknowledge these challenges upfront and approach them with patience, flexibility, and humility.

Engagement isn't just a step in a process—it's a commitment to show up, listen, and co-create in a way that honors the community's knowledge, experience, and needs.

Engagement: How do we do it?

Engagement can look different across projects—there are many ways to actively involve communities, and there's no one-size-fits-all solution. The important thing is just to start. For us we try to focus on K-Gray, making sure that we do our best to intentionally incorporate every person in the community in our involvement.

For the work that I do, engagement often looks like this:

1. We identify a community of interest.
2. We conduct a community profile.
3. We develop a key stakeholder list
4. Then we identify one major stakeholder, like a community-based organization, a local nonprofit, or a civic group that can help rally community members and who also can help design the programming
5. Then we work on co-creation.

Co-creation through engagement is often the most challenging part of the work because it requires everyone to be on the same page with a shared mission and shared objectives.

For us, this means developing a clear set of processes and protocols that all partners agree to follow from the beginning. In our work, co-creation looks like this:

1. We always start with a conversation. We bring our ideas to community leaders, and more importantly, we ask for their recommendations, critiques, and guidance on how they would like to move forward. This includes guidance on how to hold the initial conversation itself.
2. Next, we work together to develop a Memorandum of Understanding (MOU) and a scope of work. These documents clearly outline the roles and responsibilities of everyone involved. This step is critical because it protects all partners and sets clear expectations from the start.
3. We then establish a series of planning meetings. At least one of these meetings is held in person whenever possible to ensure alignment and relationship building. Every planning meeting includes an agenda, guiding documents, deadlines, and clearly defined action items.
4. Depending on the type of event or program, we work alongside the community to co-develop handouts, flyers, evaluations, supply lists, giveaways, and any additional materials needed to successfully host the event.
5. As we prepare for launch, we co-develop implementation guides and run-of-show documents. We hold pre-event meetings to ensure that every team member understands their role, their responsibilities, and how to move confidently on the day of the event.
6. Finally, we co-develop contracts for vendors and day-to-day staff. This ensures that expectations are clear, responsibilities are understood, and everyone involved is operating from the same information.

Over the years, I have learned that this 6-step process is integral to launching successful initiatives, programs, and events. Examples of our tools that we use to plan can be found in Chapter 7 and will be covered in detail in Chapter 5: Empowerment.

How will you Co-Create Engagement in the Future?

Chapter 5. Empowerment through Education.

As Chief of Staff under the Biden-Harris Administration, I saw firsthand the impact that empowerment via capacity building and fiscal investment could have on small and historically overlooked communities.

Politics aside, and regardless of how one feels about former President Biden, in my humble opinion, his administration took the time to listen. They intentionally redirected significant funding in a bipartisan way to communities that needed it most.

Under this administration, vulnerable communities across the United States gained access to training and funding that supported cleaner air, water, and soil. New infrastructure projects were launched, and grant dollars were awarded to community-based organizations that had spent decades fighting for resources to address the devastating footprints of large corporations in their neighborhoods. In many ways, this administration worked to support the little man.

I know this not from reports or headlines, but from firsthand experience. I was able to help deliver checks, sit in training, and listen to the stories of people who were desperate for both physical and financial change in their communities.

Whether you agreed with the policies or not, one thing is certain: this administration believed in engagement and empowerment, and it showed where and how capacity building and resources were distributed.

Unfortunately, we live in a world where political, economic, cultural, and social landscapes are constantly shifting. As these changes unfold, many communities are left to fend for themselves, often facing increased risks to life, health, and property.

Where governments fail to respond, leaving gaps in protection and support, like-minded organizations and individuals are often called to step in and fill the void.

Yet even with the best intentions, actions meant to help can sometimes unintentionally hinder the very communities they aim to serve, especially the world's most vulnerable populations. Which is why its so important for empowerment through education, it is imperative.

I've seen this firsthand. Early in my work, I co-created a program on behalf of a large organization. My role was to design a curriculum, secure supplies, secure staffing, and implement the program on the day of. In our haste, I realized that we had overlooked a crucial element: training!!!

When it was time to implement the program, everyone, and I mean everyone, had to come to me for direction. This was so stressful.

> *I was running around like a chicken with its head cut off because I did not do a good job in ensuring people knew what to do, how to do it, and when to do it.*

The truth is, I hadn't taken the time to empower the staff, the volunteers, or other key stakeholders who were working diligently to make the programs a success. This is actually a pretty common downfall of program managers – we often keep everything in our head, and we never write it down or train others on how to pick up the mantel so to speak.

I knew if I wanted to become a better program manager, then I had to shift my approach if I wanted the following events to be successful. I began to train everyone from the local stakeholders, providing toolkits, resources, guidance, and pre-event meetings.

As a result, our events began to flow much better, we built trust and camaraderie, and the community was no longer just a recipient of aid; they became the drivers of their own change, empowered with everything they needed to be successful.

Have you ever heard that old Chinese proverb, "Give a man a fish, and you feed him for a day; teach a man to fish, and you feed him for a lifetime." Well, its true if you just keep telling people what to do without empowering them with the skills and resources, then they will always need to rely on you. However, if you take the time to teach and build capacity, then when you leave (and eventually you will) they can continue growing and implementing the work without you.

This is the essence of empowerment through education: it's not about giving people money or surface-level solutions; it's about giving them the tools, knowledge, and confidence to make their own decisions and create lasting change. Through this approach, we can help communities move from surviving to thriving.

Bringing it all together: Steps to Program Management

Few people ever take the time out to explain the process of program management, and in this next section, I want to provide you with a breakdown of how I curate programs after I have listened and engaged with key stakeholders.

Lets start with the basics, here are the steps that I take:

It all begins with defining the scope and purpose. I clearly outline what the program will do, who it's for, and what everyone's responsibilities are. Think of this as the roadmap—it sets the course for success.

I learned this lesson the hard way. Early in my career, I jumped into a project without clear agreements. Confusion spread, expectations clashed, and it became a struggle to keep people on the same page.

Now, I make sure every stakeholder—employees, volunteers, contractors—has a written document (i..e MOU, Scopes of Works, Contracts) outlining roles, responsibilities, and expectations. Every stakeholder, employee, volunteer, contractor, service provider, or equivalent should have some written documentation that explains their roles and responsibilities. It should outline everything you can think of to prevent disagreements in the future. It should be signed and countersigned, ensuring that all parties receive a copy.

Once the roadmap is clear, it's time to plan the program. I often start by breaking it into manageable steps, setting deadlines, assigning tasks, and creating a budget. I've learned that programs can quickly become overwhelming if you try to tackle everything at once.

Breaking tasks into bite-sized pieces keeps everyone moving forward. I often use program management software like Asana to manage all of the to do list of the programs. Again, its about comfortability and adaptability. Ask the stakeholders what their preferred tool is and adapt to their preferred tool if necessary. You want to have an easy tool that can be used to manage the project's progression.

Transparency in budgeting is just as important — no hypothetical numbers here. "Don't just say give me your dream wish list items." Don't just talk factiously; use real numbers, be transparent, and show people the budget they are working with so they can plan accordingly. Do your best not to make too many exceptions, have a system, and stick to it. Transparency is key here.

Be direct. Lay out the numbers, explain the limits, and set expectations. When everyone understands the resources they have to work with, it makes planning smoother and prevents misunderstandings later.

Budgeting can be tricky at times. It's essential to be crystal clear about what funds are available — and to put it in writing. I've worked with community organizations that have operated on very limited budgets in the past, and I've seen how that can operate with a "nickel-and-dime" mentality, where every penny becomes a source of stress.

Reporting is important here as well. We use a digital bookkeeping software like QuickBooks or Wave to manage our books and reporting. Our books are then checked by a bookkeeper and an accountant to ensure that we are meeting budgetary requirements. The worst thing you can do is not account for every dollar you are given. You should be able to print out a report if asked what you did with the money.

Next, I move on to creating materials. I prepare handouts, slides, flyers, and supply lists — everything the team and community will need to participate fully. Over time, I've learned to turn these materials into reusable templates and store them in shared folders so everyone has easy access.

Another neat strategy we use is Amazon Wish List. We will share a Wishlist on Amazon and ask the community stakeholders to build out the list with items they would like to purchase. We often encourage the community leaders to choose things they can reuse again and we will donate these items back to them via in-kind donations.

I also make sure to check which platforms people are comfortable using, some may be new to computers, while others have strict firewalls or advanced systems—and adjust as needed. I often will put everything in Google Drive or a OneDrive folder and share it with all necessary stakeholders so we can be consistent. Flexibility is key.

Then, I work with the stakeholders to secure resources. We do this by ensuring we have secured the venue, supplies, volunteers, transportation, and any other essentials. Here I try to involve the stakeholders as much as possible, making sure they have autonomy in choosing their preferred venue, their volunteers and staff members.

While I do my best to ensure the stakeholders have autonomy …

> *I quite frequently will ensure that I have my own core staff members, operational supplies, and backup plans for implementation so we can jump in where necessary.*

In this field, nothing is perfect; there will always be mistakes, challenges, and things that fall through the cracks. However, if you are prepared, then you can easily reassess, or a team member can pick up the slack where necessary.

Training and preparing the team is next. walk the team through the objectives and assign roles that match each person's strengths. Everyone knows how to move with confidence. I cross-train team members so that if someone can't perform their role, someone else can step in. Guest speakers and presentations have backups, too. The goal is that the show goes on, no matter what.

Next, we implement the program. I typically will develop a clear run of shows and program guidance. We will have a meeting the day before the event to make sure the entire team is on the same page.

The day of I usually arrive about an hour early, I will pray over the place, pray for my team, and every person who will enter the door.

I label areas, assign roles, and make sure the logistics team is in place. I check for hazards and address them as much as possible. I always have a first-aid kit on hand and extra paper towels in case there are accidents or spills.

When the staff and volunteers arrive, they follow their assignments, and everything begins to flow. Years of trial and error taught me to be flexible; even with perfect planning, surprises happen, but when the process is in place, adjustments are simple.

When challenges with staff or volunteers arrive I do my best to course correct privately and directly. Over the years, I have learned that communication is key, but being clear and direct is imperative. Be sure to have written guidelines for your staff and volunteers outlining their workplace expectations. At the end of the day, they are a representation of your leadership. Teamwork makes the dreamwork.

Unfortunately, there will be times when you have to end a relationship. Learn to be okay with that—every relationship isn't meant to last forever. Feelings may get hurt, disagreements will happen, but it's important to stay true to yourself. Clear and honest communication is key. Not everyone will always be happy with your decisions, but as long as you are doing what you know is right, that's what truly matters.

Finally, we monitor and adjust.

A teammate or I will observe and check engagement. Staff will periodically walk the floor to address hazards, spot disengaged participants, and ensure the environment is welcoming. We will do our best to make real-time changes to ensure a successful event.

Every step—from defining scope to observation—is a chance to empower. It's more than checking boxes; it's about giving people the tools, confidence, and agency to act for themselves. When done well, education becomes empowerment, and empowerment becomes lasting change. Check out chapter 7 for examples of real tools and resources we use to implement our community-centered programming.

Notes

Chapter 6. Drive Change

In everything we do, our ultimate goal is to drive change. But driving change is more than just good intentions—it's about creating measurable impact, sustaining that impact over time, and finding ways to scale successes so they reach more people and communities.

Driving change starts with evaluation. We must know what's working and what isn't. This means observing outcomes, collecting feedback, and being honest about the results. Evaluation is not about pointing fingers or assigning blame; it's about understanding the effectiveness of our actions so we can improve.

For many people, evaluation is often the least favorite and hardest part of implementation. This is because it can be taxing if the right process is not put into place and the right people are not on your team. Evaluation requires careful thought, recruitment, data analysis, and reporting, which is what we will cover in the next section.

Careful Thought

Often, when we receive funding from large donors or assignments from corporations, we are asked to measure the impact or success of the program. Sometimes, the funders are the ones who have clear, measurable ideals on how they view success. Here are some examples of things I have been asked to collect in the past:

Participants Reached and Retained: Total number of individuals served, including demographic and geographic representation aligned with target populations. (i.e. 500 total people reached in Montgomery, Alabama 50% Asian American and 50% African American). Participant Retention can be described as the percentage of participants who completed the program or attended multiple sessions.

Here is an example table to illustrate how to track targeted participants. Targeted participants are those you would like to serve.

Total # of Individuals targeted (N)	% By Region	% by Gender	% by Race	% below poverty	% by Age

Why does this matter: A few years ago, I worked on a project where I was deployed into a community to conduct surveys assessing levels of damage, impact, and recovery following a major disaster. My role was to engage with nonprofit organizations to understand where support was needed so services could eventually be delivered more effectively.

When I asked some smaller nonprofits about the demographics of the populations they served, the most common response was, "We are the hands and feet of Jesus. We turn no one away; everyone is welcome." Now, I love Jesus and have no issue with faith-based service. What I do take issue with is that response.

As I sat in those rooms, I could see photos of congregations on the walls. It was clear that many of these organizations primarily served older adults or communities that were predominantly of one race or background. Yet, because they could not or would not name who they were serving, I had no way to document it.

Sometimes we become so attached to the idea that we serve everyone that we fail to examine who we are <u>actually</u> reaching.

At the end of the day, if you do not collect data on who you serve, how can you truly know whether you are reaching your intended audience or meeting the needs you claim to address?

Now, here is an example table to illustrate how to track participants reached. Reached participants are people who actually came out to your event.

Total # of Individuals Reached (N)	% By Region	% by Gender	% by Race	% below poverty	% by Age

Why does this matter: this matters because when we hold events, we don't always attract a diverse group of people, especially if we hold it in one part of town and only recruit in areas and on platforms that are typically available to certain groups.

For example, if you are a large nonprofit in a big city, you are typically going to use your corporate-approved listservs and platforms to recruit participation. You are most likely going to hold the event at your top-tier building located on the complete other part of town, away from vulnerable communities. As a result, you are not going to have a high turnout from groups that don't look, sound, or think like you.

Small local nonprofits in a big city, will typically recruit in their communities; they will use social media, canvassing, hang flyers, word of mouth, and text messaging to recruit participation. They are most likely going to hold the event at a very small and localized community center. They may have a bigger turnout, but may not be as organized as the larger nonprofit. But could you imagine if the large nonprofit teamed up with the small nonprofit, how much larger and better their impact would be?

> *The truth is you have to meet people where they are, and sometimes in the corporate world, we get caught up in the pretty shiny that we forget there are still people in the world who don't have cell phones, who have never used a computer, and when a disaster happens, they have no social networks.*

How will you reach those people if you never knew that your events never reached them?

Access and Equity: Access and equity are critical because participation only matters if people can actually show up and engage. This requires being intentional about where and how programs are delivered.

We must ask practical questions such as:

- Where are events being held?
- Is there free and accessible parking?
- Is the location impacted by heavy traffic or difficult transit routes?
- Are there added costs for participants?
- Are translation or interpretation services available?
- Is there a balance between technology-based and non-technology-based options?

Why does this matter: Each of these considerations directly affects who can participate and who is unintentionally excluded. When addressed thoughtfully, they become measurable indicators of impact that can be documented and reported back to funders and clients as evidence that barriers were identified, reduced, or removed.

Notes

Table 1. Measuring Access and Equity in Programs

Equity Dimension	Key Question	Indicator or Metric	Data Source	Measurement Method	Reporting Use
Location Accessibility	Can participants physically reach the event location?	Proximity to public transit; free parking availability; ADA compliance	Site assessment; participant feedback	Pre-event site review; post event survey	Demonstrates geographic access
Transportation Barriers	Are transportation challenges reduced?	Availability of parking, transit options; ride support	Site checklist; sign-in survey	Observation; participant self report	Equity in attendance
Cost to Participate	Is the program financially accessible?	Registration fee; hidden costs; materials provided	Budget; registration forms	Cost analysis	Financial equity
Language Access	Are language needs addressed?	Translation or interpretation offered; multilingual materials	Program materials; surveys	Document review; attendance tracking	Linguistic inclusion
Technology Access	Can participants engage regardless of digital access?	Non digital options offered; tech support availability	Program design records	Observation; participant feedback	Digital equity
Scheduling Equity	Does timing support participation?	Event timing; weekday vs weekend; duration	Registration data; feedback forms	Attendance trends analysis	Time based access
Childcare and Caregiving	Are caregivers supported?	Child friendly options; caregiver accommodations	Program notes; surveys	Self reported feedback	Care equity
Cultural Relevance	Is the program culturally appropriate?	Community input incorporated; trusted messengers used	Planning records; interviews	Qualitative review	Cultural responsiveness
Safety and Comfort	Do participants feel safe and welcomed?	Perceived safety; comfort level	Post-event survey	Likert scale questions	Inclusive environment
Participation Representation	Who is attending versus the intended audience?	Demographic alignment with the target population	Registration and surveys	Demographic comparison	Equity gap identification
Accommodations	Are disability needs addressed?	Accessibility accommodations provided	Accommodation requests	Tracking and follow-up	Disability inclusion
Community Voice	Are community members shaping decisions?	Community leadership involvement	Meeting notes; MOUs	Process documentation	Shared power

Engagement Level: Engagement level can be described as the extent of active participation, measured through attendance, discussion involvement, and hands-on activities.

Why does this matter: This measure is critical because it allows you to assess whether your events, programs, and initiatives are truly engaging before word spreads within the community and that the experience was ineffective or uninteresting, discouraging future participation.

To support this, we use a structured observation table to track engagement across events. As discussed in Chapter 5, a designated team member actively moves through the space during implementation to observe participation and make real-time adjustments when needed.

Notes

Table 2. Measuring Live Engagement

Engagement Indicator	What to Observe	Engagement Level Scale	Observation Notes	Time Stamp	Action Taken (if any)
Attendance and Retention	Participants arrive on time and remain throughout	Low; Moderate; High			
Attention and Focus	Eye contact; note taking; device use related to the activity	Low; Moderate; High			
Verbal Participation	Asking questions; contributing to the discussion	Low; Moderate; High			
Non Verbal Engagement	Nodding, smiling, body orientation toward the speaker	Low; Moderate; High			
Activity Participation	Active involvement in exercises or group work	Low; Moderate; High			
Peer Interaction	Talking with peers; collaboration	Low; Moderate; High			
Responsiveness to Facilitator	Responds to prompts or instructions	Low; Moderate; High			
Energy Level	Overall energy in the room	Low; Moderate; High			
Comprehension Indicators	Asks clarifying questions; completes tasks correctly	Low; Moderate; High			
Emotional Engagement	Displays enthusiasm; personal storytelling	Low; Moderate; High			
Disengagement Signals	Side conversations; leaving early; visible frustration	None; Some; Frequent			
Accessibility Barriers Observed	Language; hearing; vision; mobility issues	None; Minor; Significant			
Facilitator Adaptation	Adjustments made to increase engagement	Not Needed; Needed; Implemented			

Knowledge Gain, Skill Development, Behavioral Change, and Participant Satisfaction: This category looks at whether people actually learned something, felt confident using it, and were willing to take action. It helps us understand if the program moved beyond butts in chairs and information sharing into real understanding and application.

> *Remember, successful program management is not just about getting butts in chairs – it's about sparking knowledge and creating lasting intergenerational change!*

We measure changes in knowledge using pre- and post-assessments. We do this because "its not enough to get butts in chairs, we need to ensure that every person who enters can obtain and apply the knowledge they attained.

Something to note is that most workshop participants are not fond of questionnaires and there are many other ways to measure learning. You can check out this website www.betterevaluation.org for ideas to conduct your evaluation.

I usually stick with the old-school method of pre- and post-assessment, but I encourage you to develop your own strategy that meets your clients' goals. Video testimonials are also a good tool that can be used here because you can extract information in participants own voice, plus funders and clients love to connect real people to real data.

I also encourage participation, with small incentives, such as usable gifts like disaster kits or recovery buckets. To do this effectively, I typically assign a paid staff member to review and collect evaluations, while also distributing food and incentives to participants.

We observe whether participants can explain or demonstrate new skills; and we ask people directly if they feel more confident and ready to apply what they learned in real-world situations.

We also look for evidence of future action, such as participants using the tools provided, putting plans into place, or sharing information with others. Participant satisfaction is included as well, because it matters whether people felt respected, heard, and that the experience was worth their time. This also helps us figure out how to tailor our future events.

Notes

Table 3. Sample Evaluation Questions

Category	Sample Questions	Measurement Method
Knowledge	1. What are the key steps to prepare for a disaster? 2. Can you identify at least three local resources for emergency support? 3. Explain the main safety procedures for your household.	Pre- and post-assessment quizzes; multiple choice or short answer
Attitude	1. How confident do you feel in your ability to respond during an emergency? 2. How important do you feel it is to involve your family in disaster planning? 3. Rate your level of agreement: "I believe I can make a difference in my community's preparedness."	Likert scale (1–5) pre- and post-assessment
Preparedness	1. Have you created or updated a family emergency plan since this program? 2. Have you gathered any emergency supplies in your home? 3. Are you able to locate and use local emergency resources if needed?	Self-reported behavior checklist; follow-up survey
Skills	1. Demonstrate how to use a fire extinguisher correctly. 2. Show how to safely shut off water, gas, or electricity in an emergency. 3. Explain how to communicate your location and needs to emergency responders. **4. Willingness:** How willing are you to apply these skills in real-life situations?	Observation during hands-on exercises or simulations; skill demonstration checklist; self-reported willingness scale
Participant Satisfaction	1. How relevant was this program to your needs? 2. Did the program respect your experience and culture? 3. How likely are you to recommend this program to others?	Likert scale (1–5) or short-answer evaluation form; optional video testimonial

To support this work, I use the K.A.P.S. model to curate curriculum and measure knowledge change. For a deeper explanation, readers can reference: The Hazard Mitigation Training for Vulnerable Communities. Check out chapter 7, for example, a pre-post test you can tailor for your events!

Community Capacity Building: Strengthening of local organizations, leaders, or volunteers through training and collaboration. If you made it this far in this book you know that I am a big component of community capacity building and this is actually a measurable impact. I already explained in Chapter 5 how you can empower the community members you worked with so I won't go into great detail about empowerment. I'll illustrate some things you should measure so you can effectively report back.

Notes

Table 4. Leadership Evaluation Questionnaire

Capacity Area	Sample Questions / Indicators	Measurement Method
Leadership Skills	1. How confident are you in leading community initiatives after this training? 2. Have you applied any new leadership strategies learned in this program?	Pre- and post-training self-assessment; observation during exercises
Organizational Skills	1. Have you implemented any new processes or procedures from the training? 2. Are your team members more effective in completing tasks?	Follow-up survey; progress reports from the organization
Volunteer Development	1. How prepared do you feel to mentor or guide new volunteers? 2. Have volunteers increased engagement after applying new strategies?	Observation: volunteer retention and participation metrics
Collaboration & Networking	1. Have you established new partnerships or strengthened existing relationships? 2. Are you actively participating in joint initiatives with other organizations?	Network mapping, meeting attendance, and collaborative project documentation
Resource Management	1. Are you using tools, templates, or resources from the program effectively? 2. Have you improved efficiency in budgeting, planning, or reporting?	Staff feedback; review of organizational records or reporting efficiency
Sustainability & Capacity Growth	1. Has your organization increased its ability to plan and implement programs independently? 2. Are you able to train others in your organization or community?	Follow-up assessment, number of training courses conducted internally; qualitative interviews

Table 5 Capacity Building Metrics

Capacity Building Metric	Definition / What to Count	Notes / Tips
Number of Capacity Building Workshops Held	Count every workshop, training, or session designed to strengthen organizations, leaders, or volunteers.	Include in-person, virtual, and hybrid sessions.
Number of Community Leaders Trained	Count all leaders who attend and complete a capacity-building session.	Include board members, nonprofit directors, and grassroots organizers.
Number of Volunteers Trained	Count volunteers who participated in training programs aimed at increasing skills or knowledge.	Track by session and by unique individual.
Number of Organizations Engaged	Count all local organizations that participated in training, workshops, or collaborative projects.	Useful for reporting reach.
Number of Training Hours Delivered	Total cumulative hours of training provided across workshops and sessions.	Helps quantify the intensity of capacity-building efforts.
Number of Resources Shared	Count handouts, toolkits, templates, guides, or digital materials provided to participants.	Include both digital and printed resources.
Follow-up Support / Coaching Sessions Provided	Count individual or group follow-ups offered to support the implementation of skills learned.	Includes mentoring, office hours, and consultation sessions.

Sustainability and Continuation: Evidence that program activities, tools, or approaches continue beyond the funding period. This step is often critical for securing grant funds or new contracts. Funders want to know that after providing starter funds, you can maintain, grow, and leverage them.

There's an old parable from the Bible in Matthew 25 that illustrates this perfectly. A master gives his servants some money: two invest it wisely and see a return, while one buries the money out of fear of losing it.

Unsurprisingly, the two who invested reap rewards, and the one who buried the money gains nothing. Funding opportunities work the same way — funders want to see that you will take an informed risk and build on what they provide.

I tell my coaching clients all the time: everything in life comes with risk, but what you are willing to risk determines the size of your return. Stop waiting for the "perfect" opportunity and start leveraging the opportunities that are already in front of you.

Notes

Table 6. Sustainability and Continuation

Sustainability Metric	What to Measure / Count	Notes / Tips
Programs Continued Post-Funding	Count programs, workshops, or initiatives that continue after initial funding ends.	Include both fully independent and partially supported programs.
Tools / Resources Still in Use	Track toolkits, guides, or curricula that organizations continue using.	Can include manuals, software, templates, or checklists.
Local Leadership / Staff Maintaining Activities	Number of trained leaders, staff, or volunteers who are still implementing activities independently.	Helps measure knowledge transfer and capacity retention.
Partnerships Maintained	Count ongoing collaborations with community organizations, government agencies, or funders.	Indicates network sustainability.
Replication or Scaling	Count instances where program components were replicated in other communities or scaled up within the same community.	Shows program adaptability and broader impact.
Funding Leveraged / Secured	Track new funding, grants, or donations obtained to continue program activities.	Demonstrates financial sustainability.
Participant Engagement Continued	Measure if participants return for additional programs or continue using skills learned.	Shows sustained community interest.

Recruitment & Execution

Okay, recruitment and execution are integral to driving change. For us in this model, it comes down to hiring the right people, selecting the right volunteers, and ensuring the right people attend your events, initiatives, and programs. Let me break this down for you...you cannot succeed unless you have the right people to support you. I can easily say that I took $650,000 and turned it into over 25 programs in three years but guess what?!! I DID NOT DO IT BY MYSELF! I had people who believed in me who signed up to volunteer and became key staff members. Just like the ole' saying it takes a village to raise a child - well, it takes a village to launch a successful program or an initiative. Don't let people lie to you and say they do it by themselves; it's impossible to do anything by yourself and succeed without stressing yourself out!

Remember, teamwork makes the dreamwork. On my team, I usually have core staff, which consists of the following roles:

- *Program Manager (Usually Me):* The Program Manager oversees the entire program from concept to completion. This role is responsible for setting the vision, defining the scope and purpose, managing timelines and budgets, coordinating stakeholders, and ensuring all components align with the program goals. The Program Manager serves as the primary point of contact, makes final decisions when challenges arise, and ensures the program is implemented with integrity, accountability, and care for the community.

- *Program Assistant:* The Program Assistant supports the Program Manager with day-to-day coordination and administrative tasks. This includes scheduling meetings, preparing documents, tracking action items, communicating with stakeholders, and assisting with logistics. This role helps keep the program organized and moving forward smoothly.

- *Bookkeeper/Accountant:* The Bookkeeper or Accountant manages all financial aspects of the program. This includes tracking expenses, processing payments, managing invoices, reconciling budgets, and ensuring compliance with funding requirements. This role supports transparency and accountability and helps ensure funds are used appropriately.
- *Marketing Expert:* The Marketing Expert is responsible for promoting the program to the intended audience. This includes developing marketing strategies, creating promotional materials, coordinating outreach efforts, and ensuring messaging is clear, culturally appropriate, and aligned with the program's goals.
- *Social Media Expert/Intern:* The Social Media Expert or Intern manages online engagement across platforms. This role creates and schedules posts, captures photos or videos when appropriate, responds to inquiries, and helps amplify the program's reach. They also support storytelling by highlighting participant experiences and program impact.
- *Day-of-Support Staff Member:* The Day-of-Support staff member assists with real-time needs during the event or program implementation. This role helps troubleshoot issues, support staff and speakers, manage transitions, and ensure the day runs smoothly. They serve as an extra set of hands wherever support is needed.
- *Logistics Team Lead:* The logistics team lead manages all physical and operational details. This includes setting up the space, coordinating supplies, managing equipment, overseeing room flow, and ensuring accessibility needs are met. Their work ensures the environment is safe, functional, and welcoming.

- *Registration Lead:* The Registration Lead manages participant check-in and attendance. This role welcomes participants, confirms registration, distributes materials, and serves as the first point of contact. They help set the tone for the event and ensure accurate attendance records are maintained.
- *Gift Distributor/Evaluation Lead:* This role is responsible for distributing incentives, food, or giveaways and collecting completed evaluations. They help ensure participants complete feedback forms and understand their importance, supporting both engagement and evaluation goals.
- *Volunteers:* Volunteers support various aspects of the program based on need. Their roles may include setup and breakdown, participant assistance, guiding attendees, distributing materials, or supporting facilitators. Volunteers play a critical role in extending capacity and strengthening community involvement.
- *Evaluation Team*
    - *Observer:* The Observer monitors participant engagement, group dynamics, and overall flow of the program. This role looks for signs of confusion, disengagement, safety concerns, or opportunities for improvement and communicates observations to the Program Manager so adjustments can be made in real time.
    - *Quantitative Evaluator:* The Quantitative Evaluator is responsible for measuring what can be counted and tracked. This role focuses on collecting and analyzing numerical data such as attendance numbers, demographics, pre and post assessment results, survey responses, and output metrics tied to funder or client requirements. The Quantitative Evaluator ensures data collection tools are clear, accessible, and culturally appropriate, and that data is analyzed

accurately and reported in a way that demonstrates measurable impact, progress, and outcomes.

- *Qualitative Evaluator:* The Qualitative Evaluator is responsible for capturing the stories behind the numbers. This role focuses on lived experiences, perceptions, and insights gathered through interviews, focus groups, open-ended survey questions, observations, and testimonials. The Qualitative Evaluator listens for themes, patterns, and community voice, documenting how participants experience the program and what the program truly means to them. This role ensures community perspectives are centered and translated into findings that add depth, context, and meaning to quantitative results.

Selecting Vendors

Depending on the type of event that is being held, we may also recruit community-based vendors to table and provide resources to the community. In addition to the paid vendors, we have a core set of vendors that we use and stick with as much as possible. At times, we will acquire recommendations for local vendors from our community partners and use those recommendations as much as possible. However, we have developed a list of criteria that local vendors should meet before they officially become a vendor. See chapter 7 for a Vendor Vetting Checklist.

Here are a list of paid vendors we usually have at each one of our events:

- *Photographer:* Responsible for capturing high-quality photos of the event, including participant engagement, speakers, activities, and overall atmosphere. Photos are used for reporting to funders, marketing, documentation, social media, and future outreach. The photographer should understand consent, cultural sensitivity, and when photography is or is not appropriate.
- *Videographer:* Records event footage, interviews, testimonials, and highlights for reporting, training materials, and future outreach. Video content is often required by funders and useful for long term storytelling and documentation.
- *Caterer:* Provides food and beverages for participants, staff, speakers, and volunteers. Catering should account for dietary restrictions, cultural preferences, allergies, and food safety standards. Food often plays a key role in attendance, comfort, and community building at events.
- *Graphic Designer:* Creates visual materials such as flyers, social media graphics, banners, signage, handouts, and presentation templates. A strong designer ensures materials are clear, accessible, culturally appropriate, and aligned with brand guidelines.
- *Paper Print Shop:* Handles the printing of physical materials, including flyers, agendas, evaluations, worksheets, posters, and signage. Printers must meet deadlines, ensure high quality, and accommodate last-minute changes when needed.
- *Graphics Print Shop:* Produces branded T-shirts, tablecloths, banners, and other promotional materials used for visibility, professionalism, and brand recognition. These items help create a cohesive event experience and are often reused across programs.

- *Security:* Ensures the safety of participants, staff, and vendors. Security personnel help manage crowd flow, respond to incidents, and create a safe and welcoming environment, especially at large or high-traffic events. Anything over thirty to forty people we suggest hiring an off-duty officer to support the event.
- *Interpreter or Translator:* Provides language access services for participants who speak languages other than English or require ASL interpretation. This is critical for accessibility, equity, and meaningful participation. We often have at least one person on our team who is multilingual.
- *AV Technician:* Manages sound systems, microphones, projectors, screens, and lighting. A skilled AV technician ensures speakers can be heard clearly and presentations run smoothly.
- *Venue Rental Provider:* Supplies the physical space for the event, including access to rooms, seating, restrooms, parking, and utilities. Venue vendors may also provide tables, chairs, and basic setup.
- *Equipment Rental Company:* Provides tables, chairs, tents, stages, heaters, fans, generators, or other equipment needed to support the event setup.
- *Transportation Vendor:* Supports participant or staff transportation, including buses, vans, or ride services. Transportation access can significantly impact attendance and equity.
- *Cleaning or Janitorial Services:* Handles pre-event setup, cleaning, and post-event breakdown to ensure the space is left in good condition and meets venue requirements.

- *Childcare Provider:* Offers on-site childcare services so caregivers can attend events. This can be a critical access support for community participation. We will often have a "Kids Korner" just to ensure that the entire household can have equitable opportunities to increase their knowledge and build their skills.
- *Wellness or Health Services Provider:* Provides first aid, mental health support, or wellness services during events, particularly for disaster-related or high-stress programming.

Marketing

Marketing is a critical component of any program, workshop, or initiative. The way you design your marketing materials can either attract or deter your target audience. Consider not only the visuals and messaging but also the platforms you use to reach people. Social media, Eventbrite, word of mouth, text messaging, and e-mail campaigns all reach different segments of your audience and can help ensure diversity and inclusivity.

Marketing efforts are also measurable impact indicators that can be tracked and reported back to funders, investors, and clients. For example, you can monitor engagement rates, registration numbers, click-through rates, or inquiries generated from each channel. This data helps demonstrate the effectiveness of your outreach and informs future strategies.

Equally important is collaboration with your clients or partners to ensure all marketing materials are cobranded and meet their requirements. Clear communication and approvals prevent conflicts, maintain professional relationships, and ensure your materials align with the mission and values of all stakeholders.

Table 7. Community Marketing and Outreach Strategy

Target Audience	Platforms and Locations	Type of Marketing	Why This Works	Key Benefits
Community Members and Households	Facebook; Instagram; Neighborhood Listservs; Community Email Blasts; Grocery Stores; Libraries	Social Media Posts; Listserv Announcements; Printed Flyers; In-Store Postings	Reaches residents where they already receive information and gather locally	Increases awareness; Improves turnout; Strengthens community trust
Residents in Target Neighborhoods	Door-to-Door Canvassing; Community Centers; Apartment Complexes	Canvassing; One-on-One Outreach; Flyers	Personal engagement increases participation and reduces access barriers	Builds relationships; Reaches residents without internet access; Improves equity
Youth and Young Adults	Instagram; TikTok; YouTube	Short Videos; Reels; Peer to Peer Sharing	Youth prefer visual and mobile-friendly content	High engagement; Organic sharing; Strong message retention
Parents and Caregivers	Facebook; Email Lists; WhatsApp Groups; School Listservs	Event Announcements; Resource Posts; Reminder Emails	Trusted communication channels for families	Encourages attendance; Improves preparedness knowledge; Builds reliability
Educators and Schools	Email; Canvas; School Listservs; District Newsletters	Digital Flyers; Announcements; Classroom Sharing	Schools use structured systems for communication	Direct access to families; Credible endorsement; Repeat engagement
Nonprofits and Community Organizations	Email; LinkedIn; Organization Listservs	Partner Promotion; Shared Graphics; Co-Branded Messaging	Leverages trusted messengers within the community	Expands reach; Builds collaboration; Reduces outreach costs
Businesses and Vendors	LinkedIn; Email; Business Networks	Cross Promotion; Vendor Outreach; Sponsorship Highlights	Vendors and businesses benefit from visibility and goodwill	Strengthens partnerships; Increases event resources; Mutual benefit
Event Attendees and General Public	Eventbrite; Organization Website	Event Listings; Eventbrite Tagging; Partner and Vendor Tagging	Event discovery tools increase visibility beyond existing networks	Higher registrations, improved tracking; Easier reminders
Media and Influencers	Email; Instagram; X	Press Releases; Story Pitches; Visual Content	Amplifies community stories and impact	Broad visibility; Credibility; Increased public engagement
Local Government and Agencies	Email; Public Meetings; LinkedIn	Formal Invitations; Briefings; Flyers	Aligns with formal communication norms	Institutional support; Long-term sustainability; Policy alignment

Table 8. Measurement, Tracking, Evaluation Metrics, and Reporting

Outreach or Program Area	Measurement Method	Key Metrics Collected	Data Collection Tool	Tracking Frequency	Reporting Use
Social Media Marketing	Platform analytics	Reach; Impressions; Engagement; Clicks	Platform Insights Dashboards	Weekly	Grant reports; Marketing performance summaries
Listserv and Email Outreach	Email tracking	Open rate; Click through rate; Number of recipients	Email marketing platform or manual log	Per campaign	Outreach effectiveness; Audience reach
Canvassing and In Person Outreach	Field tracking	Doors knocked; Conversations held; Flyers distributed	Canvassing log or sign in sheet	Per event	Equity assessment; Community reach
Grocery Store and Physical Postings	Location tracking	Number of locations posted; Flyer lifespan	Posting log with photos	Monthly	Visibility documentation; Community access
Partner and Vendor Promotion	Partner reporting	Number of partners promoting; Shared posts	Partner confirmation emails or screenshots	Per event	Partnership impact; Collaboration metrics
Eventbrite Registration	Registration analytics	Registrations; Attendance rate; No show rate	Eventbrite dashboard	Per event	Attendance reporting; Demographic analysis
Event Attendance	Sign in tracking	Total attendees; Demographics; Repeat participants	Sign in sheets or QR check in	Day of event	Participation tracking; Equity metrics
Knowledge and Skill Outcomes	Pre and post assessments	Knowledge gain; Skill improvement	Surveys; Paper assessments	Per program	Outcome reporting; Program effectiveness
Participant Engagement	Observation tools	Engagement levels; Participation behaviors	Observation checklist	Day of event	Quality improvement; Facilitator feedback
Participant Satisfaction	Post event evaluation	Satisfaction rating; Relevance; Value	Surveys; Comment cards	Per event	Grant reporting; Program refinement
Capacity Building Outputs	Activity tracking	Workshops held; Leaders trained; Volunteers engaged	Program activity log	Quarterly	Capacity building documentation
Sustainability and Continuation	Follow up monitoring	Continued use of tools; Program replication	Follow up surveys; Interviews	3 to 12 months post program	Sustainability reporting; Future funding
Financial Accountability	Budget tracking	Cost per participant; Spend rate	Financial ledger	Monthly	Fiscal reporting; Contract compliance

Execution, Analysis, & Reporting

Measuring impact and analyzing data are critical steps in executing programs effectively and responsibly. This phase moves the work beyond implementation and into accountability, learning, and improvement.

Through intentional data collection and analysis. We track both qualitative and quantitative data to understand how our programs affect lives. Are people learning new skills? Are they more confident in their decisions? Are communities safer or better prepared? These are the questions that show whether our efforts are making a real difference.

Execution and analysis also ensure transparency with funders, partners, and the community by clearly documenting outcomes, lessons learned, and areas for growth. When done well, this process strengthens trust, supports sustainability, and positions programs to scale with integrity rather than assumption.

While I won't go into great detail about how to perform analysis or execute, there are a plethora of methods you can use to evaluate and analyze. As I said earlier, we use the K.A.P.S. method for our curriculum development, implementation process, and evaluation. If you're interested, you can purchase the book "Hazard Mitigation Training for Vulnerable Communities."

Here are some pointers to help guide the process. First, always begin with the end in mind. Ask yourself what story you are trying to tell and why it matters. Be clear about the outcomes you want to demonstrate and who the audience for that story is—funders, partners, community members, or internal staff. Next, honestly assess the depth of evaluation and analysis you are willing and able to perform. Not every program requires a complex evaluation framework, but every program does require intentionality. The level of data you collect should align with your capacity, budget, timeline, and reporting obligations. Being realistic at the outset allows you to design an evaluation process that is both meaningful and sustainable, rather than burdensome or performative.

The final point I will leave you with is the importance of establishing an evaluation team early in the process so they can support you from the beginning. As mentioned earlier, my team typically includes a qualitative evaluator, a quantitative evaluator, and someone dedicated to writing and compiling reports. When these roles are clearly defined and in place early, data collection, analysis, and reporting become more streamlined. Having a dedicated evaluation team allows you to execute efficiently, respond to issues in real time, and produce clear, credible findings that reflect the true impact of your work.

Reporting & Scaling

After you have completely moved through the evaluation process and your program has concluded. It's important to look at methods to sustain impact after your funder/client leaves. Sustaining impact is just as critical as any other item that I have described in this book.

Remember: Change that fades as soon as the program ends isn't real change. That's why we focus on empowering communities, building local leadership, and providing tools that allow people to continue the work long after we step away.

When we discover a program that works, we don't just celebrate it and move on—we look for ways to replicate it in other communities, adapting for local contexts while keeping the core principles intact.

Sustaining and scaling a program does not happen by accident. It is something I think about from the very beginning, long before the first workshop is held or the first dollar is spent. I always start by asking myself whether the work we are designing can live beyond the funding period and beyond me. If the answer is no, then something needs to change in the design.

For me, sustainability begins with intention. I build practical programs that use existing community assets and can continue even when resources are limited. I document everything—what worked, what did not, who it worked for, and why. You cannot sustain a program if you cannot clearly explain its value. Data, stories, observations, and participant feedback all become part of the record that shows the work is worth continuing.

I am also very intentional about funding. Relying on a single grant is risky. Sustainability often comes from a mix of funding sources—grants, contracts, sponsorships, earned income, and in-kind support. Funders want to know that their dollars are not the only thing holding the program together. They want to see that you have a plan to keep going once their role ends.

Another critical piece is ownership. I work to embed programs into existing systems such as schools, nonprofits, faith-based institutions, city departments, or community hubs. At the same time, I focus on training local leaders, staff, and volunteers so the work does not depend solely on me. When people feel ownership, they protect the program and help carry it forward.

Scaling comes later, and only after the program has proven itself. Not everything should be scaled. I take time to identify the core elements that make the program effective and make sure those pieces stay intact. From there, I develop toolkits, curricula, templates, and facilitator guides that allow the work to be replicated while still leaving room for adaptation to different communities.

I never scale all at once. I pilot in new spaces, learn from those experiences, and refine the approach before expanding further.

Partnerships are key here. Scaling is rarely a solo effort and working with organizations that already have trust and reach allows the impact to grow without overextending capacity.

At the end of the day, sustaining and scaling both require the same foundation: strong evaluation, clear outcomes, thoughtful risk-taking, and a willingness to invest what has been entrusted to you. Funders are not just asking whether you completed the work. They are asking what you built, who it serves, and whether it can stand on its own. That is the story sustainability and scale are meant to tell.

Reflect on a Time You had to Pilot a New Space. Did you Learn any Lessons?

Chapter 7: Lessons Learned & The L.E.E.D. With Joy Toolkit

L.E.E.D. With Joy is not just a philosophy; it is a practice. It is the accumulation of lessons learned through trial, error, community trust, missed steps, hard conversations, and moments where things went right because the groundwork was laid early. This toolkit exists so you do not have to learn everything the hard way.

I have designed, managed, and evaluated programs across communities with different levels of capacity, funding, trust, and readiness. No two spaces are the same, but the systems that support effective community work are consistent. This chapter offers both reflection and structure—what I've learned and the tools I use to do the work well, ethically, and sustainably.

The remaining portion of this book is divided into two sections: (1) Lessons I Learned the Hard Way and (2) Templates Every Program Manager Needs.

If you enjoyed this book, share it with a friend and send us your testimonials and positive reviews! Remember, my definition of success is knowing I put a smile on your face.

With Love,

Dr. Joy Semien

The Diary of A Program Manager: Lessons Learned

Be Authentically You

When I served as Chief of Staff at the EPA, I often found myself in trouble—not the kind that gets you fired, but the kind that comes with "high-level professionalism" conversations. I had never worked in government or at a corporate level before. I was fresh out of school, and while I had held jobs in the past, I had never stepped into a role that senior.

I did my best to follow all the unwritten rules—how to dress, how to speak, how to interact—because I didn't want to rock the boat. But no matter how hard I tried, I was rocking the boat every single day. I spent about three weeks trying to force myself to fit into a world that felt unfamiliar and uncomfortable. Every day, I went home frustrated, venting to my mom about how I was, once again, "in trouble."

One day, I finally gave up trying to be someone I wasn't. I told myself, if I'm going to get in trouble anyway, I might as well enjoy my day. That was the moment I returned to my "why" and reconnected with my God-given purpose. I stopped shrinking myself and started showing up as who I truly was.

> *I chose joy. I chose curiosity. I asked questions, built relationships, laughed, and made other people laugh. I leaned fully into my authenticity.*

By the end of my tenure, the same spaces that once felt rigid were filled with laughter and connection. I may not have fit the traditional mold of corporate professionalism, but I was good at my job—and more importantly, I loved going to work every day.

There were hard moments and plenty of growing pains, but that role became one of the best experiences of my career. It taught me that authenticity is not a liability—it is a strength. When you show up as yourself, you not only do better work, but you create space for others to do the same.

Lesson Learned: Always be authentically you. People will not always like you, and they will not always agree with you—and that is okay. Authenticity is not about pleasing everyone; it is about operating in alignment with your values and your God-given purpose. When you lead from that place, you move with clarity, confidence, and conviction. You become grounded in who you are and why you are doing the work. That alignment is what makes you unstoppable—not because the road is easy, but because you are no longer trying to be someone you are not.

Know Your Why

I opened this book with that very phrase—telling you my why. If I know nothing else, I know who I am and whose I am. When you know your why, everything you do becomes grounded in purpose. On the hard days, or in moments when quitting feels like the easier choice, your why is what keeps you moving forward. Remember, there are people who need your smile, your wisdom, and your love. Lean into your why, and let it guide everything you do.

Lesson Learned: Knowing your why is like having a compass for your work. When challenges arise or doubt creeps in, your purpose keeps you focused and motivated. Grounding your actions in your why allows you to persevere and have a meaningful impact, even when others don't see it.

Owning Your Knowledge

When I was in school pursuing one of my degrees, a friend and I worked on a project that eventually got published in an academic journal—an achievement anyone in academia would recognize as a big deal. We brought in two other collaborators to support the project, and early on, we all agreed on authorship order. But just a few hours before the final submission, one coauthor decided that I didn't deserve second place—despite it being my friends' and I's idea, my paper, and the majority of the groundwork.

I was ready to protest, but after talking with my mentors, I made the difficult decision to…

> *let it go—not because I didn't want that recognition, but because it wasn't worth the fight at that moment.*

I took the loss—or the "L," as the younger generation might say—and walked away.

What I learned from that experience was invaluable: I needed to protect myself and my work. That moment pushed me to understand trademarks, copyrights, and patents. I began proactively involving lawyers whenever I created something.

Today, I hold trademarks, copyrights, and have published over 20 books—and counting. While it was a hard lesson to learn, taking the L gracefully allowed me to make better decisions for my future.

Lesson Learned: Always protect your ideas and intellectual property. Recognition is important, but safeguarding your work ensures you can continue creating without fear of losing credit or ownership. Taking a temporary loss can lead to long-term gain if it teaches you how to defend your contributions professionally.

Speaking up

In recent years, I've learned the importance of advocating for my worth. When I first started my companies, I often did work for free or at a reduced cost, thinking it would help build relationships and opportunities. What I didn't realize was that this approach ended up costing me significantly — I remember one year I lost over $65,000 simply because I didn't stand up and ask for what I deserved.

Since then, everything has changed. I've learned to clearly articulate my value, write detailed scopes of work, create contracts, and involve lawyers when necessary. I've also learned how to use the rule of three when collecting payment for my work: *Initial Deposit, Draft Payment, and Final Payment.*

> **Business isn't a place for timidity—if you let others dictate your worth, you will be taken advantage of.**

I now know when to give and when to say, "Enough is enough." I honor my hard work, my time, and my contributions, and I make sure others do too.

Lesson Learned: Never underestimate your value. Protect your time, expertise, and resources by speaking up, setting clear expectations, and establishing boundaries. Your work is worth it, and advocating for yourself is essential to long-term success. Remember No is a complete sentence – don't overwork yourself to please others. They will just replace you if you can't complete the task.

Navigating Corporate America

This was a hard lesson for me. Most of my work had been in communities, and I quickly learned that community members and leaders operate very differently from corporate America. The first time I had the opportunity to work on a corporate project, I immediately realized the learning curve ahead.

Corporate environments move on a completely different timeline. There's often a strict hierarchy with multiple levels of approval. At times, decisions are slow and methodical; at other times, things move lightning fast, with information demanded on their schedule—regardless of your own commitments.

I quickly realized I had to establish strong boundaries. I had to stand firm in my "no's," communicate clearly, mean what I said, and say what I meant.

I had to be confident in who I was and what I was capable of, without wavering under pressure.

Lesson Learned: Corporate and community spaces operate differently, and success requires self-awareness, clear communication, and strong boundaries. Know your capacity, assert your limits, and honor your expertise—doing so ensures you maintain respect and effectiveness across both worlds.

Trust But Verify

I can't emphasize this enough: trust but always verify. I've worked on countless projects where people confidently said, "Don't worry, I've got this," only for things to fall apart on the day of the event. Supplies went missing, teams were in the wrong rooms, and speakers didn't show up.

Over time, I learned the hard way that verbal agreements aren't enough. No matter how much you trust someone, always get it in writing. Confirm responsibilities, timelines, and expectations in clear, documented formats. Don't micromanage but perform quality checks to ensure the program will go off without any obvious hitches. This small step can prevent chaos, confusion, and unnecessary stress during your programs.

Lesson Learned: Do your due diligence. Trust your team but protect your work. Remember: Written agreements, checklists, and confirmations are not signs of distrust—they are the tools that ensure your vision becomes reality.

Conflict Management

Let me be very clear: people will be people. You can't control personalities, how others perceive you, or how situations unfold.

> *The only thing you can control is being authentically you—and when conflicts arise, taking deliberate steps to address them head-on.*

I remember one situation where I was constantly butting heads with a coworker. No matter what we tried, we just couldn't see eye to eye. Finally, we scheduled a meeting to talk openly about the issues that were causing tension. What we discovered was eye-opening: we were both misreading each other, jumping to conclusions, and, because we were rushed, we were talking past one another instead of solving anything.

We decided to reset. Using many of the strategies I outline in this book—active listening, clear communication, and setting expectations—we were able to reduce misunderstandings and work together more effectively.

Lesson Learned: Conflicts are inevitable. What matters is how you respond. Approach disagreements with honesty, authenticity, and a willingness to reset. When you do, you protect your relationships, your work, and your peace of mind.

Picking Your Battles & Knowing Your Worth

A few years ago, I had the opportunity to work with someone I had admired for years. I looked up to this person and respected the work they did in the community. At first, everything seemed perfect—but over time, I discovered that this same person had begun talking behind my back, telling others in the community that working with me was "difficult" or "problematic." At no point did they come to me directly to share their concerns.

The truth is, my work was impeccable. I received glowing reviews from both clients and community members. But their desire to move in a different direction led them to degrade me instead of communicating openly. Initially, I wanted to defend myself and confront them, but after speaking with a mentor, I realized that some battles weren't worth the fight. I knew my worth, I knew what I was capable of, and I chose to let my future work and projects speak for themselves.

I also took proactive steps to protect myself moving forward.

In all future contracts, I included a defamation clause, ensuring that clients could be held accountable if they attempted to tarnish my name or work without evidence.

Lesson Learned: Protect your reputation and your work. Not everyone will communicate honestly, and sometimes people will try to bring you down. Stand firm in your worth, choose your battles wisely, and take practical steps—

like legal protections—to safeguard your name and your professional integrity. Remember: *Let the Haters Hate and protect your peace!*

Pivoting & Backup Plans

I once worked on a year-long project where we were responsible for providing speakers at community events. Early on, I learned the hard way that some speakers would wait until the day of the event to cancel—or worse, simply not show up. It was frustrating, stressful, and could have derailed the events entirely.

I quickly learned how to pivot. I began developing backup PowerPoints and resources in case a speaker didn't appear. I implemented multiple confirmation emails—one a week before, one the day before, and even one the morning of the event. I also started prioritizing highly recommended or paid speakers, ensuring greater accountability and reliability.

Lesson Learned: Always plan for the unexpected. No matter how well you organize, people will let you down. Having a backup plan—whether that's substitute speakers, extra materials, or contingency activities—ensures the event continues smoothly and your audience still gets a meaningful experience. Flexibility and preparation are your best tools in managing uncertainty.

Handholding Might be Imperative

I once worked with a small nonprofit that, at first glance, seemed extremely competent. They appeared ready to handle tasks independently, and I trusted them to execute. However, after a few months, it became clear they needed hands-on guidance and support for every step of the process.

At first, I was frustrated, but I quickly realized this is okay. Some partners—especially smaller community organizations or newer team members—need more support to build their confidence and skills. I took the time to walk them through each step, explaining, modelling, and checking in regularly. Over time, they became self-sufficient and capable of achieving success independently.

Lesson Learned: Don't expect everyone to arrive fully prepared. Take the time to guide, mentor, and support your partners. Patience and hands-on guidance can transform initial struggles into lasting capacity and confidence. The investment pays off when those you support can eventually take ownership and thrive on their own.

Maintaining your Own Core Staff

I once worked with a small business that asked us to curate a series of workshop programs. They assured me they could provide staff to support the events. But when the day finally arrived, none of their staff showed up, leaving me to handle everything myself.

It was a stressful moment, but it taught me an important truth: no matter what clients promise, you need to have your own core team in place to ensure the program runs smoothly. I relied on my trusted staff to step in, and we were able to execute the event successfully.

Lesson Learned: Always maintain a reliable core team and treat client or partner staff as supplemental support. At the end of the day, the show must go on, and your team is your safety net.

Security and Medical Support Persons are Key

I once attended an event with more than one hundred people, and the level of chaos was unimaginable. Exits were blocked; aisles were cluttered with materials and people; the AV equipment was so poor that attendees were talking over the main speaker; and there was no one designated to manage the confusion. Just when it seemed things could not get worse, someone spilled liquid in a hallway. Before the staff could clean it up, an older woman slipped and nearly did splits across the puddle. Thankfully, she was not seriously injured, but the situation could have ended very differently.

Lesson Learned: Sometimes we get so caught up in hosting an event that we overlook critical support needs. That experience led me to establish a firm rule for my company. Any event with more than thirty-five participants must include either a medical support person and/or security. We also ensure a fully stocked first aid kit is always on site. Planning for safety is not optional; it is a responsibility.

Friendships and Business

When I was first starting, I relied heavily on my friendships to help fill many of my staff roles due to limited physical and fiscal support. That may be the case for you, too, especially if you operate, but I want to offer some guidance so you can protect both your work and your relationships.

Some friends own businesses and are more than capable of supporting your vision and bringing professionalism to the table.

While some friends should never be brought into your business or made partners, because they struggle to separate friendship from work. Knowing the difference matters.

To protect yourself and your friendships, it is important to have clear, written contracts and scopes of work. Only ask friends to support roles they are qualified for, and have an honest conversation upfront about expectations, responsibilities, timelines, and compensation. Once those boundaries are set, do your best not to drift outside of them.

Lesson Learned: Treat friends who are working with you the same way you would treat any other employee or vendor. That clarity protects everyone involved. If the arrangement is not a good fit, they will let you know, and it is better to learn that early than to lose a relationship later.

These are just some of the lessons I have learned over the last twenty years of program management. 😊 Over that time, I've experienced triumphs and setbacks, successes and failures, and each moment has shaped the way I approach my work today.

From navigating complex community dynamics to managing teams, budgets, and logistics, every challenge has been an opportunity to grow, refine my skills, and strengthen my purpose. These lessons are not just tips—they are guiding principles that have helped me lead with joy, stay true to my values, and make an impact in the communities I serve.

The L.E.E.D. With Joy Toolkit

Guide: Supporting Community-Based Organizations in Starting Their Own Business or Nonprofit

Purpose:

This guide is designed to help program managers support community-based organizations (CBOs) that may not yet have formal structures such as a 501(c)(3) nonprofit or an LLC. A lack of official paperwork should never prevent a CBO from being a valuable stakeholder. As a program manager, you can guide these organizations in establishing their own legal entity, setting up operational systems, and preparing for sustainable growth.

Disclaimer:

The information in this guide is provided as recommendations only. For professional legal or financial guidance, always consult a licensed lawyer or accountant.

Steps to Start a Business or Nonprofit

1. Decide on a Name
   - Choose a unique and meaningful name for your organization or business. Ensure it aligns with your mission and vision.

2. Choose Your Type of Company
   - Options include LLC, PLLC, Partnership, S Corp, C Corp, or Nonprofit Organization. Talk to a lawyer for recommendations.

3. File with Your State
   - Visit your state's Secretary of State's office to file the necessary paperwork to become an entity in your state. Every state is different, so be sure to talk to a lawyer for recommendations.

4. Obtain Federal Identification Numbers

Employer Identification Number (EIN)
- **What it is:** The EIN is like a Social Security number for your business or nonprofit. It identifies your organization for tax purposes and is required for things like opening a business bank account, hiring employees, and filing taxes.

- **How to get it:** You apply directly with the IRS, either online, by phone, fax, or mail.

- **Cost:** Free.

- **Tips:** Apply as soon as you legally form your business or nonprofit. Even if you don't have employees immediately, it's good to secure an EIN to separate personal and business finances.

Beneficial Ownership Information (BOI) Filing
- **What it is:** This filing, required by the Financial Crimes Enforcement Network (FinCEN), identifies the individuals who own or control a legal entity. It's part of federal efforts to prevent fraud, money laundering, and other illegal activities.

- **How to file:** Submit your BOI filing through FinCEN's online portal.

- **Cost:** There is no fee for filing.

- **Tips:** Keep your ownership information updated. If there are changes in your leadership or ownership structure, update your BOI filing within the required timeframe.

DUNS Number (Data Universal Numbering System)
- **What it is:** The DUNS number is a unique nine-digit identifier for your business used by Dun & Bradstreet. It's often required to apply for government grants, contracts, and certain business services.

- **How to get it:** You can register for a DUNS number through the Dun & Bradstreet website.

- **Cost:** Free for most nonprofit and government-related applications.

- **Tips:** Make sure your organization's legal name, address, and contact information are consistent across all registrations to avoid delays.

5. Open a Business Bank Account
   - Keep personal and business finances separate.
   - Consider business credit cards: (i.e. Amex, Chase, Capital One)
   - Open a payment processing account/system (i.e. Stripe, Paypal, etc.)

6. Define Services and Revenue Streams
   - Create a list of services or items to sell
   - Establish prices for products/services

7. Branding
   - Take professional headshots
   - Develop a professional website, e-mail account, and phone number
   - Design a professional logo
   - Set up business social media accounts (i.e. Tiktok, Facebook, Instagram, LinkedIn, link.tree)

Key Lesson:

Even without formal paperwork, CBOs can be trusted, valued stakeholders. Supporting them in building their legal and operational foundations strengthens the community and allows them to sustainably scale their impact. With clear steps and structured guidance, program managers can empower these organizations to grow, protect their work, and achieve their mission.

Table 9. Operational Tools & Platforms

Tool/Platform	Purpose	Tips & Notes
Website Platforms: Wix, Shopify, Etsy	Host your business online, sell products, and provide information to clients.	Wix for general websites, Shopify for e-commerce, Etsy for handmade or niche products. Keep your site user-friendly and mobile-friendly.
Logo: Canva	Create a professional logo and branded graphics.	Use templates to maintain consistency across social media, flyers, and merchandise. Keep it simple and memorable.
Social Media Pages: Instagram, Facebook, LinkedIn	Promote your business, engage clients, and build community.	Use Instagram for visuals, Facebook for community engagement, LinkedIn for professional networking. Schedule posts and interact with followers regularly.
Business Email: Gmail	Professional communication with clients, vendors, and stakeholders.	Consider Google Workspace for added tools like Drive and Calendar. Keep your email separate from personal accounts.
Virtual Business Number: Google Voice	Separate business communications from personal calls and texts.	Forward calls if needed, maintain clear work hours, and share the number publicly for clients.
Payment Services: PayPal, Stripe, Square, CashApp, Zelle, Clover	Accept online and in-person payments securely and efficiently.	Choose platforms that align with your clients' preferences. Keep records of all transactions for accounting purposes.
Accounting Software: QuickBooks, Sage, Wave	Track expenses, revenue, taxes, and generate financial reports.	Wave is free for basic use, QuickBooks and Sage offer more advanced features. Keep accounts updated regularly to avoid end-of-year stress.
Digital Business Card: HiHello	Share professional contact information quickly and digitally.	Can include website, social links, and email. Great for networking and reducing paper waste.
Business Insurance: Hiscox	Protects your business from liability, property damage, or unforeseen events.	Review coverage based on business type and activities. Helps protect your assets and maintain credibility with clients.
Review Platforms: Yelp, Google	Collect and showcase client reviews to build credibility.	Regularly check for reviews, respond professionally, and encourage satisfied clients to leave feedback.
Organize Workflow / To-Do Lists: Asana, Google To-do list, Microsoft Word To-do list	Track tasks, deadlines, and project progress for yourself and your team.	Use the platform that best fits your workflow. Set reminders and update tasks daily to stay organized.
Intake Forms: Jotform	Collect client, participant, or vendor information efficiently.	Design forms to capture necessary data clearly and securely. Integrate with email or database systems if needed.

Community Listening Checklist

Purpose: Use this checklist to understand a community's context, priorities, and needs before designing programs or initiatives. The goal is to listen first, engage authentically, and build solutions that resonate. Remember, listening is not a one-time activity. Return to the community regularly, validate what you heard, and adjust your program based on ongoing input.

1. Understanding the Community

- What makes this community unique? (Culture, history, traditions)
- Who are the formal and informal leaders?
- What local organizations, groups, or networks already exist?
- What strengths, skills, and assets does the community have?
- What are the community's current challenges or barriers?
- Are there past programs or initiatives we can learn from?

2. Community Needs and Priorities

- What issues matter most to the people living here?
- How do community members define success or positive change?
- What gaps exist in services, resources, or opportunities?
- Are there hidden needs or voices that are often overlooked?

3. Engagement and Participation

- Who should be involved in co-creating this program?
- How does the community prefer to share their thoughts? (Meetings, interviews, surveys, informal conversations)
- How can we ensure inclusivity for historically marginalized voices?

- What supports or incentives do participants need to engage fully?
- Are there barriers that might prevent participation (time, transportation, trust, language)?

4. Context and Environment

- What physical or geographic factors influence community life?
- Are there environmental or infrastructure considerations we need to know?
- Are there local policies or regulations that affect program implementation?
- How does the community interact with nearby communities or regions?
- Are there historical experiences (positive or negative) with programs, funders, or officials?

5. Building Trust and Relationships

- How can we show respect for the community's expertise and lived experience?
- How will we communicate decisions, progress, and challenges?
- How do we ensure transparency and accountability?

6. Reflection and Action

- What are the key insights we heard from the community, and how can these insights inform the design of the program?
- How will we involve the community in decision-making and ownership?
- What steps will we take to ensure the program is sustainable and not temporary?

Key Stakeholder Map

Purpose: Use this table to outline who are the key stakeholders in your community. Be sure to identify their name, organization, Contact Information, and the type of stakeholder. The goal is to make a list of anyone who may be useful to in ensuring the event will go off without a hitch!

Stakeholder Type	Organization Name	Point of Contact Name	Phone #	E-mail	Address

Stakeholder Letters

Purpose: Use these letters to invite community stakeholders to work with you in launching the event.

Letter to a Community Leader

Subject: Partnering to Co-Create a Community Initiative

Dear [Community Leader's Name],

I hope this message finds you well. I am reaching out to share an exciting opportunity to work together on a new initiative designed to support [community name] in addressing [specific issue or opportunity].

At the heart of this work is listening and learning from those who know the community best—you and your neighbors. We hope to collaborate with you as a co-creator to design a program that reflects the community's priorities, strengths, and needs.

Your insights, experience, and leadership are critical to ensuring this initiative is meaningful and impactful. I would love to schedule a meeting at your convenience to discuss how we can work together and hear your perspective.

Thank you for your time and for all you do for the community. I look forward to the possibility of partnering with you.

Warm regards,
[Your Name]
[Title / Organization]
[Contact Information]

Letter to a Government Official

Subject: Collaboration Opportunity for Community Initiative

Dear [Official's Name],

I hope this note finds you well. I am reaching out to inform you about a new initiative focused on [specific community or issue] in [community/location]. This program is designed to be community-led and solutions-focused, and we hope to engage your office as a partner.

Your perspective and support are invaluable in ensuring that the initiative aligns with existing policies, resources, and programs while addressing the real needs of residents. We would greatly appreciate the opportunity to share more about the initiative and discuss ways we might collaborate to maximize impact.

Please let me know a convenient time for a brief meeting or call. Thank you for your time and consideration, and for your commitment to the communities you serve.

Sincerely,
[Your Name]
[Title / Organization]
[Contact Information]

Letter to a Local Business

Subject: Partnering to Support [Community Initiative]

Dear [Business Leader's Name],

I am excited to share a new community initiative focused on [specific issue or opportunity] in [community]. This program is designed to be community-driven, empowering residents and local organizations to take part in shaping solutions that matter most.

Local businesses like yours play a critical role in creating sustainable impact. We would love to explore ways your organization could support this initiative—whether through sponsorship, in-kind contributions, volunteering, or other forms of collaboration.

I would be happy to schedule a time to discuss this initiative in more detail and explore opportunities to work together. Thank you for your consideration and for all you do to strengthen our community.

Best regards,
[Your Name]
[Title / Organization]
[Contact Information]

Letter to Community Members

Subject: New Initiative Launching in [Community Name]!

Dear [Community Member's Name],

We are excited to announce a new initiative in [community] focused on [specific goal or issue]. This program was created with you in mind—your voice, your needs, and your experience are central to its design.

We want to hear from you! Your input will guide how the program is implemented, ensuring it is practical, relevant, and meaningful for everyone. We invite you to attend [meeting/event/workshop] on [date] at [location] to share your thoughts, ideas, and priorities.

Together, we can create solutions that reflect the community's strengths and meet its needs. Thank you for being part of this important effort!

Warm regards,
[Your Name]
[Title / Organization]
[Contact Information]

Letter to Vendors

Subject: Partnership Opportunity with [Initiative Name]

Dear [Vendor's Name],

I am reaching out to share an exciting opportunity to support a new initiative focused on [community or issue]. As we plan and implement this program, we are looking to partner with vendors who can provide [specific products/services] to help make this initiative successful.

We value collaboration, clear communication, and timely delivery, and we would love to discuss how your organization could be involved. Please let me know a convenient time to connect and explore opportunities for partnership.

Thank you for your time and consideration. I look forward to the possibility of working together.

Sincerely,
[Your Name]
[Title / Organization]
[Contact Information]

Letter to Suppliers

Subject: Supply Partnership Opportunity for [Initiative Name]

Dear [Supplier's Name],

I hope this note finds you well. We are in the process of launching a new initiative focused on [community or issue], and we are seeking suppliers to provide [specific materials/products] that will help bring this project to life.

Your expertise and quality products are critical to ensuring the program is successful and sustainable. We would love the opportunity to discuss how we might work together, including timelines, quantities, and other partnership details.

Thank you for considering this opportunity. I look forward to connecting and exploring how we can collaborate.

Best regards,
[Your Name]
[Title / Organization]
[Contact Information]

One-on-One Conversation Toolkit: Listening with Intent

Purpose: Use this guide to help facilitate one-on-one conversations. The guide will help you listen with intent.

- *Set the Purpose:* Begin by clearly defining why you are having the conversation. Are you gathering insights, understanding needs, or co-designing solutions? Sharing the purpose builds trust and sets expectations.
- *Choose a Comfortable Setting:* Meet in a space where the stakeholder feels safe and able to speak openly. This could be a quiet office, a local community space, or even a virtual platform.
- *Prepare Questions Ahead of Time:* Have a list of open-ended questions ready, but stay flexible. The goal is to listen and let the conversation flow naturally.
- *Start with Active Listening:* Give the stakeholder your full attention. Avoid interrupting, take notes, and show engagement through nods or affirming words.
- *Reflect and Clarify:* Periodically summarize what the person said and ask clarifying questions. This ensures you understood correctly and shows that you value their input.
- *Explore Their Perspective:* Ask about challenges, successes, needs, and priorities. Encourage them to share examples, stories, or experiences that illustrate their points.
- *Acknowledge and Validate:* Recognize their feelings and experiences. Statements like "I hear you" or "That makes sense" help build trust and make them feel heard.

- *Capture Actionable Insights:* Take note of ideas, suggestions, and potential solutions. Look for patterns or points that can inform your program or initiative.
- *Close with Next Steps:* Summarize what you learned and explain how their input will be used. Clarify any follow-up actions to show that listening leads to action.
- *Follow Up:* Send a thank-you note or message and keep them informed on progress. Maintaining communication reinforces trust and shared ownership.

Methods to Conduct Listening Sessions

Purpose: Use these sample guides to help conduct listening sessions with your key stakeholders.

One-on-One Conversations

Purpose:

To understand an individual stakeholder's experiences, priorities, and insights. This method allows for deeper, personalized engagement and builds trust.

How to Do It:

1. Set a clear purpose and share it upfront.
2. Choose a private, comfortable setting (in-person or virtual).
3. Prepare open-ended questions but stay flexible.
4. Listen actively, take notes, and reflect on what you hear.
5. Clarify points to ensure understanding.
6. Summarize key takeaways and confirm next steps.

Tips:

- Use reflective statements like "I hear you" to validate input.
- Encourage storytelling; personal experiences reveal insights numbers cannot.
- Mind your body language, tone, and presence.

Follow-Up:

- Send a thank-you message.
- Share how insights influence decisions or program design.
- Keep the stakeholder updated on progress.

Focus Groups

Purpose:

To capture group perspectives, identify common priorities, and explore differences of opinion.

How to Do It:

1. Gather 6–12 participants representing the community or stakeholder group.
2. Prepare discussion prompts and open-ended questions.
3. Facilitate the conversation, ensuring everyone has a chance to speak.
4. Record or take detailed notes.
5. Identify patterns, conflicts, and shared priorities.

Tips:

- Encourage respectful dialogue; avoid dominating the conversation.
- Use icebreakers to create a comfortable environment.
- Watch for non-verbal cues that indicate agreement or concern.

Follow-Up:

- Summarize findings and share with participants.
- Integrate insights into program design or decisions.

Community Surveys

Purpose:

To gather feedback from a large group efficiently, capturing both quantitative and qualitative insights.

How to Do It:

1. Design clear, concise questions aligned with your objectives.
2. Include a mix of multiple-choice and open-ended questions.
3. Distribute via email, social media, or in-person methods.
4. Collect and analyze results for trends and priorities.

Tips:

- Keep surveys short to increase participation.
- Offer language options if necessary for inclusivity.
- Follow up with reminders for higher response rates.

Follow-Up:

- Share results with participants.
- Use data to guide program decisions.
- Communicate how the feedback influenced outcomes.

Town Hall Meetings

Purpose:

To engage a broad audience, promote transparency, and gather collective input.

How to Do It:

1. Schedule a public meeting and announce widely.
2. Provide an agenda and context for discussion.
3. Encourage open dialogue and questions.
4. Take notes or record the meeting.
5. Identify key themes and community priorities.

Tips:

- Establish ground rules for respectful communication.
- Use visuals or handouts to support clarity.
- Provide opportunities for those uncomfortable speaking publicly to submit feedback in writing.

Follow-Up:

- Share a summary of key takeaways.
- Communicate how input will shape programs.
- Maintain ongoing engagement with participants.

Observation / Field Visits

Purpose:

To directly witness how community members interact with their environment, resources, or programs.

How to Do It:

1. Visit community spaces, schools, or events.
2. Observe behaviors, interactions, and patterns.
3. Take detailed notes or photos (with permission).
4. Identify unmet needs or challenges.
5. Supplement observations with follow-up conversations.

Tips:

- Be unobtrusive; avoid altering natural behavior.
- Document what you see, not just what you assume.
- Respect privacy and cultural norms.

Follow-Up:

- Integrate observations into planning and decision-making.
- Discuss findings with stakeholders for validation.

Co-Creation Workshops

Purpose:

To actively involve stakeholders in designing solutions, programs, or projects.

How to Do It:

1. Invite diverse stakeholders to participate.
2. Present objectives and context.
3. Facilitate exercises to brainstorm, prioritize, and design solutions.
4. Encourage collaboration and shared decision-making.
5. Document outcomes for implementation.

Tips:

- Provide materials and clear instructions.
- Create small groups for focused discussions.
- Ensure all voices are heard and valued.

Follow-Up:

- Share workshop outcomes with participants.
- Implement solutions co-created by the group.
- Recognize contributions publicly when possible.

Storytelling Sessions

Purpose:

To gather qualitative insights through personal narratives and lived experiences.

How to Do It:

1. Invite participants to share stories related to the issue or program.
2. Create a safe, supportive environment for sharing.
3. Ask guiding questions to elicit rich details.
4. Listen actively and take notes or record (with permission).

Tips:

- Encourage emotional honesty; stories reveal insights that numbers cannot.
- Be empathetic and avoid judgment.
- Connect themes across stories to identify common challenges and solutions.

Follow-Up:

- Use stories to inform program design and advocacy.
- Share anonymized stories to communicate impact.

Listening Tours

Purpose:

To hear from multiple groups and locations within a community to gather diverse perspectives.

How to Do It:

1. Plan visits to different neighborhoods, organizations, or community spaces.
2. Meet with representatives and community members in each location.
3. Ask consistent questions to compare insights across sites.
4. Document observations and key takeaways.

Tips:

- Respect local schedules and cultural norms.
- Be present and attentive in each location.
- Look for patterns and differences between groups.

Follow-Up:

- Share findings across the community and stakeholders.
- Use insights to create inclusive, place-based programs.

Advisory Committees / Councils

Purpose:

To establish a group of key stakeholders to provide ongoing guidance, feedback, and accountability.

How to Do It:

1. Identify diverse representatives from the community or sector.
2. Schedule regular meetings to discuss progress, challenges, and next steps.
3. Share updates and solicit feedback on decisions.
4. Use the committee to validate strategies and priorities.

Tips:

- Rotate membership to ensure fresh perspectives.
- Encourage open dialogue and respectful debate.
- Recognize contributions to maintain engagement.

Follow-Up:

- Implement feedback and document actions taken.
- Communicate outcomes to the broader community.

Digital Platforms / Forums

Purpose:

To gather input from stakeholders who may not attend in-person sessions.

How to Do It:

1. Create an online platform for discussion, surveys, or Q&A.
2. Encourage participation through clear instructions and prompts.
3. Monitor contributions and respond as needed.
4. Collect insights and identify key themes.

Tips:

- Ensure accessibility and ease of use.
- Moderate to maintain respectful engagement.
- Use visuals, polls, or videos to increase participation.

Follow-Up:

- Share findings with participants.
- Highlight how feedback influenced decisions or programs.

Sample Operational Agreements

This Operational Agreement ("Agreement") is entered into as of [Date], by and among the following parties:

Parties:

1. **[Party Name / Business Name]**, located at [Address]

2. **[Party Name / Business Name]**, located at [Address]
   (Add additional parties as needed)

Purpose:
This Agreement establishes the roles, responsibilities, and expectations of all parties involved in [describe purpose, e.g., "the operation and management of [Program/Business/Initiative Name]"]. The goal is to ensure clear communication, accountability, and successful execution of activities.

1. Roles and Responsibilities

Each party agrees to fulfill the following responsibilities:

Party	Role	Responsibilities
[Party 1]	[Role]	[List specific responsibilities]
[Party 2]	[Role]	[List specific responsibilities]
[Party 3]	[Role]	[List specific responsibilities]

Optional: Include timelines or deadlines for key responsibilities.

2. Decision-Making

- Decisions will be made by [describe decision-making process, e.g., majority vote, unanimous agreement, or assigned lead for specific areas].

- For urgent decisions that cannot wait for a group meeting, [Party Name] has authority to act on behalf of the group, with communication to all parties immediately after.

3. Communication

- Parties agree to maintain clear and timely communication through [email, phone, Slack, Zoom, etc.].

- Meetings will be held [frequency] to review progress, challenges, and upcoming tasks.

- All major updates, changes, or issues will be documented and shared with all parties.

4. Financial Responsibilities

- [Specify how funds, budgets, or shared costs will be handled.]

- [Specify expense approval process and reporting expectations.]

- Each party will maintain accurate records of expenditures and receipts.

5. Confidentiality

- Parties agree to maintain confidentiality of sensitive information, client data, and proprietary processes.

- Confidential information may not be disclosed to external parties without written consent.

6. Conflict Resolution

- Disputes will first be addressed through direct conversation among the parties.

- If unresolved, mediation or arbitration will be used as a next step.

- [Optional: Specify mediator/arbitration provider or rules.]

7. Termination

- This Agreement may be terminated by mutual consent of all parties.

- Notice of termination must be provided [number] days in advance.

- Obligations or responsibilities prior to termination will be fulfilled by all parties.

8. Amendments

- Changes or amendments to this Agreement must be made in writing and signed by all parties.

Signatures:

Party	Name	Title	Signature	Date
[Party 1]				
[Party 2]				
[Party 3]				

Notes / Tips for Use:

- This template is flexible for **partnerships, nonprofits, program teams, or collaborative initiatives**.

- Always customize **roles, decision-making processes, and financial sections** to reflect your specific arrangement.

- Consider consulting a lawyer if this agreement involves **funding, contracts, or liability**.

Sample Memorandum of Understanding (MOU)

Purpose: The Memorandum of Understanding outlines a collaborative partnership between the parties involved to co-create and implement community-centered programming. Each party agrees to clearly defined roles and responsibilities, open communication, and collective accountability to ensure the work is meaningful, accessible, and sustainable.

Memorandum of Understanding

This Memorandum of Understanding (MOU) is entered into on [Date] by and between:

Organization A: [Name of Organization]
Address: [Address]

and

Organization B: [Name of Community Based Organization]
Address: [Address]

Collectively referred to as "the Parties."

Purpose

The purpose of this MOU is to establish a collaborative partnership between the Parties to co create, implement, and support [brief description of program, initiative, or project]. This partnership is grounded in mutual respect, shared responsibility, and a commitment to community centered outcomes.

Guiding Principles

The Parties agree to operate under the following principles:

- Listening to community voices and lived experiences
- Shared decision making and transparency
- Mutual accountability and trust
- Cultural responsiveness and equity
- Commitment to sustainable impact beyond the project timeline

Roles and Responsibilities

Organization A agrees to:

- Provide overall coordination and project management
- Secure and manage funding, when applicable
- Support planning, facilitation, and documentation efforts
- Provide technical assistance, training, or resources as needed
- Communicate clearly and regularly with Organization B

Organization B agrees to:

- Serve as a community liaison and trusted connector
- Provide guidance based on community needs and priorities
- Assist with outreach, recruitment, and engagement
- Co design programming, materials, and implementation strategies
- Participate in planning meetings and evaluation activities

Shared Responsibilities

Both Parties agree to:

- Participate in regular planning and check-in meetings
- Share information openly and respectfully
- Address challenges collaboratively and in good faith
- Uphold agreed-upon timelines and deliverables

- Center community needs throughout the project lifecycle

Communication

The Parties agree to maintain open and consistent communication. Primary points of contact for this agreement are:

- Organization A Contact: [Name, Title, Email, Phone]
- Organization B Contact: [Name, Title, Email, Phone]

Timeline

This MOU will be effective from [Start Date] through [End Date], unless amended or terminated earlier by mutual written agreement.

Modification and Termination

This MOU may be modified at any time by mutual written consent of both Parties. Either Party may terminate this agreement with [30 or 60] days written notice.

Non-Binding Agreement

This MOU reflects the intent of the Parties to collaborate and does not constitute a legally binding contract. Any financial agreements or contractual obligations will be outlined in separate documents, if applicable.

Signatures

By signing below, the Parties acknowledge and agree to the terms outlined in this MOU.

Organization A

Name: _____

Title: _____

Signature: _____

Date: _____

Organization B

Name: _____

Title: _____

Signature: _____

Date: _____

Sample Scope of Work (SOW) – Detailed Template

Purpose: The purpose of this Scope of Work is to clearly define the objectives, responsibilities, deliverables, and timelines for all parties involved in this project. It serves as a guiding document to ensure accountability, alignment, and shared understanding, minimizing confusion and providing a roadmap for successful collaboration and program implementation.

Scope of Work (SOW) – Detailed Template

Project Title: [Insert Program/Initiative Name]
Prepared For: [Community Partner / Organization Name]
Prepared By: [Your Organization Name]
Date: [Insert Date]

1. Purpose

The purpose of this project is to collaboratively design, implement, and evaluate a program that addresses the specific needs of the community. The program will be co-created with community leaders, local organizations, and stakeholders to ensure relevance, accessibility, and impact.

2. Objectives

- Engage community members in program design to ensure relevance and cultural responsiveness.
- Provide training, resources, and support to community partners to build capacity.
- Implement the program successfully while tracking participation, satisfaction, and outcomes.

- Foster trust and long-term relationships between stakeholders and the community.
- Document lessons learned to inform future programs and initiatives.

3. Scope of Work

A. Planning & Co Creation

- Conduct introductory meetings with key community stakeholders to identify priorities and concerns.
- Co-create program objectives, activities, and materials with community leaders.
- Develop a detailed program plan including agenda, run of show, supply list, and evaluation tools.
- Co-develop Memorandum of Understanding (MOU) to outline roles, responsibilities, and expectations.

B. Community Engagement

- Identify target audience and outreach strategies with partners.
- Develop and distribute promotional materials (flyers, social media, newsletters).
- Host pre-program community sessions to ensure awareness and gather input.

C. Implementation

- Facilitate program events or workshops with community partners.
- Provide logistical support, including venues, transportation, supplies, and staffing.
- Ensure day-of coordination aligns with co-created plan.

- Monitor participation, collect feedback, and address challenges in real time.

D. Capacity Building

- Train community partners on program facilitation, data collection, and reporting.
- Provide toolkits, guides, and reference materials to support local leadership.
- Ensure that knowledge and skills are transferred to local stakeholders for sustainability.

E. Evaluation & Reporting

- Collect and analyze quantitative and qualitative data from program participants.
- Provide a summary report including outcomes, lessons learned, and recommendations.
- Share findings with all partners and funders to inform future initiatives.

4. Roles and Responsibilities

Role	Responsibility	Lead Contact
Lead Organization	Overall program coordination, funding, and reporting	[Name]
Community Partners	Outreach, co-facilitation, community insight	[Name]
Vendors / Suppliers	Provide materials, services, or products	[Name]
Evaluation Team	Collect and analyze data, summarize results	[Name]

5. Deliverables

- Co-created program plan and MOU
- Promotional materials and outreach strategy
- Implementation of all scheduled workshops/events
- Toolkit and guidance documents for community partners
- Final evaluation report including lessons learned

6. Timeline

Phase	Key Activities	Timeline
Planning & Co Creation	Intro meetings, MOU, program plan	[Dates]
Engagement	Outreach, pre-program sessions	[Dates]
Implementation	Program launch, facilitation	[Dates]
Evaluation	Data collection, reporting	[Dates]

7. Communication

- Weekly or biweekly check-ins via phone, video, or in person
- Email updates for all deliverables and action items
- Single point of contact identified for each stakeholder

8. Success Metrics

- Number of community members engaged
- Attendance at events and workshops
- Participant satisfaction and feedback
- Capacity built within community organizations
- Recommendations implemented for future initiatives

Sample Non-Disclosure Agreement (NDA)

Purpose: The purpose of this agreement is to establish a shared understanding that protects confidential information exchanged during collaboration, planning, and implementation while supporting open, honest, and trust-based partnerships.

Non-Disclosure Agreement

This Non-Disclosure Agreement (the "Agreement") is entered into on [Date] by and between:

Disclosing Party: [Name of Organization or Individual]
Receiving Party: [Name of Organization or Individual]

Purpose

The purpose of this Agreement is to protect confidential information that may be shared during discussions, planning, collaboration, or implementation of programs, initiatives, or partnerships.

Definition of Confidential Information

Confidential Information includes, but is not limited to, any non-public information shared verbally, electronically, or in writing, including program plans, funding information, strategies, data, personal information, proprietary materials, and community insights.

Obligations of the Receiving Party

The Receiving Party agrees to:

- Keep all Confidential Information private and secure

- Use the Confidential Information solely for the agreed-upon purpose
- Not disclose Confidential Information to any third party without prior written consent
- Take reasonable steps to prevent unauthorized access or disclosure

Exclusions

Confidential Information does not include information that:

- Is publicly available through no fault of the Receiving Party
- Was known before disclosure
- Is independently developed without use of the Confidential Information
- It is required to be disclosed by law or court order

Term

This Agreement shall remain in effect for [one, two, or three] years from the date of disclosure unless otherwise agreed upon in writing.

No Ownership or License

Nothing in this Agreement grants ownership or rights to the Confidential Information beyond its intended use.

Governing Law

This Agreement shall be governed by the laws of the State of [State].

Signatures

By signing below, the Parties agree to the terms of this Non-Disclosure Agreement.

Sample Copyright Release Form

Purpose: The purpose of this form is to clearly explain how materials will be used and to document permission, so everyone involved understands their rights and responsibilities.

Copyright Release and Permission Agreement

I, _____ ("Releasor"), hereby grant permission to _____ ("Releasee") to use, reproduce, publish, distribute, and display my submitted materials for lawful purposes.

Description of Materials

This release applies to the following materials (check all that apply and describe as needed):

☐ Written content

☐ Photographs

☐ Audio recordings

☐ Video recordings

☐ Artwork or graphics

☐ Other: _____

Description of Materials:

_____

_____

Grant of Rights

I grant the Releasee a non-exclusive, royalty-free, perpetual, and worldwide license to use the materials in print, digital, and electronic formats, including but not limited to books, reports, training materials, presentations, websites, and promotional materials.

Ownership

I confirm that I am the original creator and copyright holder of the materials listed above, or that I have full authority to grant this permission.

No Compensation

I understand and agree that no compensation is required or expected in exchange for this permission unless otherwise stated in writing.

Waiver of Claims

I release and hold harmless the Releasee from any claims related to the use of the materials as permitted under this agreement.

Governing Law

This agreement shall be governed by the laws of the State of _____.

Signature

Releasor Name: _____

Signature: _____

Date: _____

Address (optional): _____

Email or Phone (optional): _____

Data Sharing Agreement

This Data Sharing Agreement ("Agreement") is entered into as of [Date] by and between:

Organization/Partner A: [Name, Address]
Organization/Partner B: [Name, Address]

Purpose:
The purpose of this Agreement is to define the terms under which the Parties will share and use data to [describe project, e.g., "support community program development, evaluation, and reporting"] while ensuring privacy, confidentiality, and compliance with applicable laws.

1. Definitions

- **Data:** Any information shared between the Parties under this Agreement, including but not limited to surveys, reports, demographic information, and evaluation results.
- **Confidential Data:** Any data that is not publicly available and is shared under this Agreement.

2. Scope of Data Sharing

- The Parties agree to share data only for the purpose described above.
- Data will be used solely for program development, analysis, and reporting.
- Data ownership remains with the originating Party unless otherwise agreed in writing.

3. Confidentiality

- Each Party agrees to maintain the confidentiality of the shared data.
- Data shall not be disclosed to any third party without prior written consent from the originating Party.

4. Data Security

- Each Party agrees to implement reasonable technical and organizational measures to protect shared data from unauthorized access, loss, or disclosure.

5. Compliance

- The Parties will comply with all applicable privacy laws and regulations, including [specify local/national laws if applicable].

6. Duration and Termination

- This Agreement shall remain in effect until [end date] or until terminated by either Party with 30 days' written notice.
- Upon termination, all shared data must be returned or securely destroyed unless retention is required by law.

7. Dispute Resolution

- Any disputes arising under this Agreement shall be resolved through good faith discussions between the Parties.

8. Signatures

Partner	Name	Title	Signature	Date
Organization/Partner A				
Organization/Partner B				

Step-by-Step Guide to Running a Program or Workshop

1. Listen & Understand the Community

- *What to do:* Talk to people who live in the community. Ask what problems they face, what would help them, and what they care about.
- *How to do it:* Hold short conversations, ask questions in surveys, or meet community leaders for coffee.
- *Example:* If you want to run a health workshop, ask residents what health topics matter most to them.

2. Identify Key Stakeholders

- *What to do:* Make a list of people and groups who have a say in the community or can help your program.
- *Who this includes:* Community leaders, nonprofits, local business owners, schools, government staff, and funders.
- *Example:* A local church leader might help spread the word; a school principal might let you use their space.

3. Engage Stakeholders

- *What to do:* Invite these people to help plan the program with you. Ask for their ideas and advice.
- *Why:* Programs work better when the people they are meant to serve help design them.
- *Example:* Ask a community leader, "What day works best for people to come? What topics would be most useful?"

4. Define Scope & Purpose

- *What to do:* Write down clearly what your program will do, who it's for, and what everyone is responsible for.
- *Why:* Everyone needs to know their role to avoid confusion.
- *Example:* "This workshop will teach families how to prepare for disasters. The community leader will recruit participants, I will bring the supplies, and volunteers will help run activities."

5. Plan the Program

- *What to do:* Break the program into small steps, and make a schedule.
- *What to include:* Agenda, timelines, tasks, supplies, and who is responsible for what.
- *Example:* Decide what will happen first (welcome), middle (activities), and end (feedback).

6. Create Materials

- *What to do:* Prepare everything you will use during the program.
- *What to include:* Handouts, slides, flyers, signs, supply lists, name tags.
- *Example:* If it's a cooking workshop, prepare recipes and ingredients ahead of time.

7. Secure Resources

- *What to do:* Make sure you have all the tools, people, and places you need.
- *Examples:* Book a room, order tables and chairs, hire a photographer, get snacks, arrange transportation.

8. Train & Prepare Your Team

- *What to do:* Make sure everyone helping you knows what to do.
- *Why:* People work better when they feel confident.
- *Example:* Walk volunteers through each activity, show them the handouts, and explain how to answer questions.

9. Implement the Program

- *What to do:* Run the program according to your plan.
- *Tips:* Arrive early, check supplies, and greet everyone warmly. Be flexible if things change.

10. Monitor & Adjust

- *What to do:* Pay attention to what's happening. Ask: Are people engaged? Are activities running smoothly?
- *What to do if needed:* Make small changes on the spot.
- *Example:* If a game is too long, shorten it so participants don't lose interest.

11. Evaluate

- *What to do:* After the program, ask for feedback. What worked? What didn't?
- *How:* Use surveys, informal conversations, or observation notes.
- *Example:* Ask, "What was your favorite part?" or "What could we do better next time?"

12. Celebrate & Sustain

- *What to do:* Recognize everyone who helped. Share results with stakeholders and the community.
- *Why:* This keeps people motivated and shows the value of their work.
- *Example:* Send thank-you notes, post pictures on social media, or hold a small celebration.

Writing a Mission and a Vision Statement

Purpose: Provide clear guidance and practical steps for crafting effective mission and vision statements. These statements will help organizations and programs define their core purpose, communicate their goals, and inspire stakeholders to align with their work.

Understanding the Difference

Statement	Purpose	Focus	Timeframe
Mission Statement	Explain **why your organization or initiative exists** and what it does	Present, practical, action-oriented	Today and near-term
Vision Statement	Describes **what you aspire to achieve** in the future	Future-focused, inspirational	Long-term

Writing a Mission Statement

- **Step 1: Define your core purpose**
    - Why does your organization exist?
    - What problem are you solving or need are you addressing?

- **Step 2: Identify your audience:**
    - Who do you serve?

- **Step 3: Outline what you do**
    - What services, programs, or actions do you provide?

- **Step 4: Add your value or impact**
    - How do you make a difference?

Template Example:

"Our mission is to [what you do] for [who you serve] by [how you do it], so that [impact or change]."

Example:

"Our mission is to empower underserved communities by providing disaster preparedness training and resources, so residents can respond effectively and protect their families and neighborhoods."

3. Writing a Vision Statement

Step 1: Imagine the ideal future: What does success look like?

Step 2: Be aspirational: Think big, but realistic.

Step 3: Keep it short and inspiring: Usually 1–2 sentences.

Template Example: "Our vision is a world where [ideal future or outcome]."

Example: "Our vision is a world where every community is prepared, resilient, and empowered to thrive in the face of disasters."

4. Tips for Both Statements

- Use clear, simple language and avoid jargon.
- Keep mission practical and vision aspirational.
- Test them with your team and stakeholders to ensure alignment.
- Revisit every few years—they can evolve as your organization grows.

Writing Program and Learning Objectives Using Bloom's Taxonomy

One-Pager: Writing Program and Learning Objectives Using Bloom's Taxonomy

Purpose: This guide helps program managers and educators clearly define program objectives and learning objectives using Bloom's Taxonomy, ensuring outcomes are measurable, actionable, and aligned with participant learning and program goals.

Program Objectives vs. Learning Objectives

Type	Description	Example
Program Objectives	Broad, overarching goals of your program. Focus on what the program as a whole intends to achieve.	"Increase community disaster preparedness among 100 local families."
Learning Objectives	Specific, measurable statements about what participants will know, do, or feel as a result of the program. Use Bloom's Taxonomy verbs to make them actionable.	"Participants will be able to create a family emergency kit that meets FEMA guidelines."

Bloom's Taxonomy Levels & Action Verbs

Level	Description	Action Verbs	Example Learning Objective
Remembering	Recall basic facts or concepts	define, list, identify, recall	"Participants will list 5 items required in a family emergency kit."
Understanding	Explain ideas or concepts	describe, explain, summarize, interpret	"Participants will explain the importance of having an emergency evacuation plan."
Applying	Use information in new situations	implement, demonstrate, execute, use	"Participants will demonstrate how to turn off utilities safely during an emergency."
Analyzing	Break information into parts to explore relationships	differentiate, compare, contrast, examine	"Participants will compare different types of emergency communication plans."

Level	Description	Action Verbs	Example Learning Objective
Evaluating	Justify a decision or course of action	assess, critique, recommend, judge	"Participants will assess their current household emergency plan and recommend improvements."
Creating	Produce new or original work	design, develop, create, construct	"Participants will develop a customized disaster preparedness plan for their household."

Tips for Writing Objectives

1. **Start with an action verb** from Bloom's Taxonomy.

2. **Be specific and measurable** – avoid vague phrases like "understand" or "know."

3. **Align objectives with program goals** – each learning objective should support a program objective.

4. **Keep participants in mind** – consider what they will actually do or demonstrate.

5. **Use multiple levels** – combine lower-level objectives (remembering, understanding) with higher-level objectives (applying, creating) for a well-rounded program.

Types of Community Engagement Activities

Type	Description	Primary Purpose	Typical Format & Length	How It Can Be Interactive/Hands-On
Community Event	A one-time or short-term gathering designed to bring people together around a shared topic, resource, or celebration.	Awareness, visibility, trust-building	1–4 hours, open to the public	Vendor tables, live demos, Q&A, giveaways, polling boards
Community Information Meeting	A structured meeting used to share information, updates, or plans with residents.	Inform, update, build transparency	1–2 hours, presentation + discussion	Q&A sessions, feedback cards, live polling, comment boards
Workshop	A focused, interactive learning session designed to build specific knowledge or skills.	Skill-building, learning, preparedness	1–3 hours, facilitated	Small-group activities, worksheets, scenarios, demonstrations
Training	A structured instructional session often tied to competencies or certifications.	Capacity building, workforce readiness	Half-day to multi-day	Practice exercises, role-playing, assessments, simulations
Program	A multi-session or long-term initiative that combines events, workshops, and follow-up activities.	Sustained impact and behavior change	Weeks to months	Cohort learning, coaching, assignments, milestones
Vendor/Resource Fair	An event where organizations share services, tools, and resources with the community.	Access to services, referrals	2–4 hours, open floor	Hands-on demos, screenings, mini-assessments, sign-ups
Advocacy Event	An organized effort to educate, mobilize, or influence policy or decision-makers.	Policy change, awareness, mobilization	Rallies, forums, town halls	Story-sharing, action stations, petitions, letter writing

Type	Description	Primary Purpose	Typical Format & Length	How It Can Be Interactive/Hands-On
Town Hall	A public forum where leaders and community members engage in dialogue.	Dialogue, accountability	1–2 hours	Open mic, moderated discussion, live questions
Listening Session	A community-centered forum focused on hearing lived experiences and feedback.	Trust-building, needs assessment	1–2 hours, facilitated	Small-group conversations, story circles, note capture
Focus Group	A targeted discussion with a specific population to explore perspectives in depth.	Insight gathering, program design	60–90 minutes	Guided discussion, scenario reactions
Community Advisory Board (CAB)	A group of residents or stakeholders who provide ongoing guidance.	Shared decision-making	Ongoing meetings	Co-planning, voting, and strategy sessions
Pop-Up Engagement	Short, informal engagement set up in community spaces.	Reach people where they are	30–90 minutes	Interactive displays, quick surveys, demos
Hybrid/Virtual Event	Engagement delivered partially or fully online.	Accessibility and reach	Virtual or mixed	Breakout rooms, polls, chat engagement
Demonstration Project	A hands-on showcase of a tool, practice, or solution in action.	Learning by doing	Variable	Live demonstrations, participant trials
Train-the-Trainer Session	Prepares participants to deliver content to others.	Sustainability and scaling	Half-day to multi-day	Practice teaching, feedback loops
Community Planning Session	Collaborative sessions to co-create plans, strategies, or initiatives.	Co-creation, shared ownership	2–4 hours	Mapping exercises, visioning, group work

Introductory Meeting for Co-Creating a Program

Purpose: To build relationships, align expectations, and determine whether co-creation is the right approach for this partnership.

Who Should Be in the Room

- Community leaders or representatives
- Community-based organizations
- Project or program leads
- Funders or decision makers when appropriate

What This Meeting Is Not

- A pitch meeting
- A decision-making meeting
- A finalized planning session

What This Meeting Is

- A listening session
- A relationship-building opportunity
- A space to understand community priorities and capacity

Key Questions to Explore

- What issues matter most to this community right now
- What has been tried before, and what worked or did not work
- Who needs to be involved in this effort to succeed
- What does success look like from the community's perspective

Outcome

- Shared understanding
- Decision on whether to move forward together
- Agreement on next steps

Planning Document Overview

Purpose: To guide the co-creation process and keep all partners aligned throughout planning and implementation.

Core Components

- Program goals and objectives
- Target audience
- Roles and responsibilities
- Timeline and milestones
- Budget considerations
- Communication plan

How It Is Used

- As a living document
- Reviewed and updated during planning meetings
- Referenced during implementation

Best Practice

- Co-develop this document with community partners
- Avoid overly technical language
- Ensure everyone has access to the final version

Program Planning Document

This document serves as a comprehensive guide to assist participating organizations in planning, developing, and implementing effective programs. It provides structured guidance, best practices, and key considerations to ensure successful program execution. This document will be used as a resource to align the program initiatives with strategic goals, optimize resource allocation, and enhance community impact.

Title	Description	Cost
Workshop Title		
CBO Partner		
Workshop Date		
Workshop Time		
Location		
Target Audience		
Workshop Topic		
Workshop Theme		
Workshop Objective		
Brief Agenda Topics		
Hands-on Activity		
Day-of Handouts	Sign-in sheets, evaluations, and waiver for participation	
Giveaway		
Workshop Design/ Room Setup		
Style Tables		

# Tables		
# Chairs		
AV Needs	Microphone, speaker, HTMI, Computer, Projector Screen, projector, extension cord, internet/wifi	
Accessibility		
Key Stakeholders		
Proposed Speaker		
Speaker Gifts		
Logistics		
Staff		
Volunteers		
Food Vendors (Vegan Options)		
Community Vendors		
Marketing		
Create promotional materials	Flyers, social media posts, emails	
Use multiple channels	website, newsletters, community boards	
Set up a registration system	Eventbrite	
Confirmation E-mails	Send confirmation emails and reminders to registrants.	

Sample Planning Meeting Agenda

Meeting Title: Program Co Creation Planning Meeting

Duration: 60–90 minutes

Agenda

1. Welcome and introductions

2. Purpose of the meeting

3. Recap of community priorities and goals

4. Discussion of proposed program components

5. Roles and responsibilities

6. Timeline and key dates

7. Open discussion and feedback

8. Next steps and action items

Meeting Norms

- One person speaks at a time
- All voices are valued
- Questions and concerns are encouraged

Sample Task Timeline

Phase 1: Relationship Building and Listening

- Introductory meetings
- Community conversations
- Stakeholder identification

Phase 2: Co-Creation and Planning

- Program design sessions
- Resource and supply planning
- Outreach and marketing development

Phase 3: Preparation and Launch

- Finalize materials
- Confirm logistics and locations
- Conduct run of show meeting

Phase 4: Implementation and Reflection

- Program delivery
- Debrief with partners
- Gather feedback and lessons learned

Sample Assignment Timeline

Task	Date	Assigned Person	Completed (Y/N)

Vendor Vetting Checklist

Purpose: To ensure vendors are reliable, ethical, cost-effective, and aligned with program values, community needs, and funding requirements.

Vendor Basic Information

- Legal business name
- Primary contact person and title
- Phone number and email address
- Business address
- Website or online presence
- Years in operation

Business Legitimacy and Compliance

- Business license or registration verified
- Tax ID or W9 provided
- Proof of insurance if required
- Certifications or permits required for services provided
- Ability to meet local, state, and federal compliance requirements
- No known legal or ethical violations

Product or Service Fit

- Clear description of goods or services offered
- Products or services meet program needs and specifications
- Capacity to deliver the required quantity and quality
- Ability to meet timeline and delivery deadlines
- Flexibility to accommodate community-specific needs
- Experience providing similar services or products

Cost and Pricing

- Itemized pricing provided in writing
- Pricing aligns with budget constraints
- Transparent fees; no hidden costs
- Discounts available for nonprofits or bulk purchases
- Payment terms clearly stated
- Refund and cancellation policies reviewed

Equity and Community Alignment

- Vendor demonstrates respect for community values
- Commitment to ethical labor practices
- Cultural awareness and sensitivity demonstrated
- Community-based, Minority owned, women-owned, or locally owned business, identified if applicable
- Willingness to work collaboratively with community partners

Reliability and Performance History

- References provided and checked
- Positive reviews or testimonials verified
- History of on-time delivery or service completion
- Clear communication practices
- Responsiveness to questions or concerns

Data and Privacy Considerations (If Applicable)

- Data handling and privacy policies reviewed
- Agreement to protect participant or organizational data
- Willingness to sign NDA or data sharing agreement if required

Risk Management

- Contingency plans for delays or shortages
- Backup options identified if service cannot be fulfilled
- Clear point of contact for issue resolution

Documentation and Agreements

- Written contract or purchase agreement reviewed
- Scope of work or service agreement finalized
- Cancellation and termination clauses reviewed
- Signed and countersigned documentation on file

Final Decision

- Vendor approved
- Vendor approved with conditions
- Vendor not approved

Reviewer Name: _____

Date Reviewed: _____

Notes: _____

Vendor List

Vendor Type	POC Name	POC Phone #	POC E-mail Address	Secured

Logistics Contractor One-Pager

Purpose: The Logistics Contractor is responsible for the physical execution of event logistics. This role ensures that all materials, equipment, and supplies are safely transported, properly set up, maintained during the event, and efficiently removed after the event concludes. This position is essential to ensuring events start on time, operate smoothly, and close out safely.

Event Information

Event Name: _____

Date(s): _____

Venue Name & Address: _____

Load-In Time: _____ Event Start: _____

Event End: _____ Load-Out Time: _____

Program Manager / Point of Contact: _____

Phone / Email: _____

Logistics Contractor Information

Company / Contractor Name: _____

Primary Contact: _____

Phone / Email: _____

Number of Staff Assigned: _____

1. Scope of Logistics Responsibilities

Check all that apply:

- ☐ Load-in and unloading
- ☐ Transportation of materials
- ☐ Table and chair setup
- ☐ Vendor table setup
- ☐ Tent or canopy setup
- ☐ Signage and banner placement
- ☐ Audiovisual equipment placement
- ☐ Mid-event space adjustments
- ☐ Event breakdown and cleanup
- ☐ Transport to storage location

Additional responsibilities specific to this event:

_____

_____

_____

2. Materials and Equipment Checklist

Initial when item is loaded, set up, and removed.

Item	Quantity	Loaded	Set Up	Removed
Tables	_____	☐	☐	☐
Chairs	_____	☐	☐	☐
Tablecloths / Linens	_____	☐	☐	☐
Vendor Tables	_____	☐	☐	☐
Banners / Signage	_____	☐	☐	☐
AV Equipment	_____	☐	☐	☐
Extension Cords / Power Strips	_____	☐	☐	☐
Storage Bins / Carts	_____	☐	☐	☐
Tents / Canopies	_____	☐	☐	☐

Other materials:

_____

3. PPE and Moving Supplies Checklist

Check items available and used.

Personal Protective Equipment

- ☐ Work gloves
- ☐ Closed-toe shoes or safety boots
- ☐ Safety vest
- ☐ Back support belt
- ☐ Face mask (if required)

Moving and Setup Supplies

- ☐ Dollies or hand trucks
- ☐ Rolling carts
- ☐ Furniture sliders
- ☐ Ratchet straps or bungee cords
- ☐ Zip ties or Velcro straps
- ☐ Moving blankets
- ☐ Tool kit
- ☐ Gaffer tape or duct tape

Missing or damaged equipment noted:

4. Staffing and Task Assignment

List logistics staff and primary duties.

Staff Name Role / Task Arrival Time

_____

5. Timeline and Execution Plan

Load-In Tasks

_____

_____

Setup Completion Time

Target time setup is complete: _____

Load-Out Tasks

_____

_____

_____

6. Safety and Incident Log

Record any injuries, damage, or safety concerns.

_____

_____

_____

_____

7. Final Walk-Through and Sign-Off

- ☐ Venue returned to original condition
- ☐ All materials accounted for
- ☐ Equipment secured and transported
- ☐ No outstanding issues

Logistics Contractor Signature: _____

Date: _____

Program Manager Signature: _____

Date: _____

Logistics Contractor Training

Purpose: This training prepares logistics contractors to safely, efficiently, and professionally support events by managing the movement, setup, and breakdown of materials. Contractors are expected to operate with reliability, clear communication, and respect for timelines, venues, and community partners.

Event Setup, Safety, and Professional Standards

Contractor Information

Contractor Name: _____

Company (if applicable): _____

Phone / Email: _____

Event(s) Covered: _____

Training Date: _____

Trainer Name: _____

Role Overview and Expectations

Logistics contractors are responsible for:

☐ On-time arrival for load-in and load-out

☐ Safe transportation of materials

☐ Proper setup and breakdown of event spaces

☐ Careful handling of equipment and supplies

☐ Maintaining a clean and organized workspace

- ☐ Following instructions from the Program Manager
- ☐ Representing the organization professionally at all times

Boundaries:

Logistics contractors are not responsible for program facilitation, registration, or vendor management unless explicitly stated in the scope of work.

Safety Training and Requirements

Required Safety Practices

- ☐ Lift with proper body mechanics
- ☐ Use PPE at all times when moving materials
- ☐ Secure loads during transport
- ☐ Keep walkways clear and hazard-free
- ☐ Report unsafe conditions immediately

Required PPE

- ☐ Closed-toe shoes
- ☐ Work gloves
- ☐ Safety vest (if required)
- ☐ Back support belt (recommended)

Emergency Procedures Reviewed: ☐ Yes ☐ No

Equipment and Material Handling

Check items reviewed during training:

- ☐ Dollies and hand trucks
- ☐ Rolling carts
- ☐ Moving blankets

- ☐ Ratchet straps or bungee cords
- ☐ Tents, tables, chairs, and signage
- ☐ AV equipment placement protocols

Damage Prevention Standards:

All materials must be handled as if personally owned. Any damage must be reported immediately.

Communication and Chain of Command

Primary Point of Contact

Name: _____

Phone: _____

- ☐ Instructions come from the Program Manager or designee only
- ☐ Changes must be approved before execution
- ☐ Questions should be asked early, not during setup delays

Professional Conduct Standards

- ☐ Dress appropriately for physical labor
- ☐ Be respectful to staff, volunteers, vendors, and community members
- ☐ No use of drugs or alcohol before or during work hours
- ☐ No unauthorized guests in work areas
- ☐ Maintain confidentiality of event operations

Failure to meet these standards may result in removal from the event or termination of contract.

Time Management and Accountability

- ☐ Arrive at least _____ minutes before scheduled load-in
- ☐ Complete setup by assigned deadline
- ☐ Remain available during event if required
- ☐ Complete full load-out unless released by Program Manager

Scenario-Based Training Review

Trainer to review examples:

- ☐ Late arrival scenario
- ☐ Missing equipment scenario
- ☐ Venue access delay
- ☐ Last-minute layout changes
- ☐ Emergency evacuation procedures

Contractor Acknowledgment

I acknowledge that I have received training, understand my responsibilities, and agree to follow all safety, communication, and professional conduct expectations.

Contractor Signature: _____

Date: _____

Trainer Signature: _____

Date: _____

Training Note

Strong logistics are invisible when done well and unforgettable when done poorly. This role matters.

Example Independent Contractor Agreement

Purpose: This agreement is an example contract you can adapt to your preference when hiring independent contractors. Be sure to follow up with a lawyer so you can ensure the contract meets your organization's standards.

This Independent Contractor Agreement ("Agreement") is made and entered into as of [Date], by and between:
Company: L.E.E.D. With Joy LLC ("Company"), with principal offices at [Address]
Contractor: [Contractor Name] ("Contractor"), residing at [Address]
Collectively referred to as the "Parties."

Engagement of Services

The Company hereby engages Contractor to provide services related to [describe services, e.g., program facilitation, event support, content creation, consulting, etc.], and Contractor agrees to provide such services in a professional and timely manner.

Term

This Agreement begins on [Start Date] and will continue until [End Date] or until terminated according to Section 8 of this Agreement.

Compensation

- Contractor will be paid [rate, e.g., $XX per hour or $XXX per project] for services rendered.
- Payment will be made [weekly, biweekly, or upon completion of deliverables] via [method].
- Contractor is responsible for all applicable taxes and will not be considered an employee of the Company.

Independent Contractor Status

Contractor acknowledges that they are an independent contractor and not an employee of the Company. Contractor will not be entitled to Company benefits, and the Company will not withhold taxes on Contractor's behalf.

Work Standards & Conduct

- Contractors shall perform all services with the highest professional standards.
- Contractors shall comply with Company policies, including safety, confidentiality, and ethics.
- **Drug and Alcohol Policy:** Contractor agrees not to use or be under the influence of drugs or alcohol during work hours, on Company premises, or while representing the Company. Violation may result in immediate termination of this Agreement.

Liability and Insurance

- Contractor shall maintain general liability insurance coverage of at least [amount, e.g., $1,000,000] during the term of this Agreement.
- Contractor shall provide proof of insurance prior to beginning work.
- Contractor agrees to hold the Company harmless from any claims, damages, or losses resulting from Contractor's work, negligence, or misconduct.

Confidentiality

Contractor agrees to keep all proprietary, sensitive, confidential information, or trade secrets, learned during the term of this Agreement private and shall not directly or indirectly disclose to any person. Trade secrets include, but are not limited to: [list your items here].

This obligation continues indefinitely, even after the termination of this Agreement.

Non-Compete

During the term of this Agreement and for [e.g., 12 months] following its termination, Contractor agrees not to directly compete with the Company by providing similar services to clients, organizations, or communities served by the Company without prior written consent.

Non-Solicitation

Contractor shall not solicit the Company's clients, employees, volunteers, or partners for personal gain or on behalf of another organization during this Agreement and for [e.g., 12 months] following its termination.

Intellectual Property

- Any work, materials, or intellectual property developed by Contractor for the Company shall be the sole property of the Company.
- Contractor agrees to transfer all rights and provide assistance necessary to secure the Company's ownership of such work.

Work Product

- All materials, deliverables, and work product created, developed, or prepared by the Contractor in connection with the performance of services under this Agreement, including but not limited to reports, presentations, templates, curricula, designs, data, research, software, graphics, or other intellectual property (collectively, "Work Product"), shall be the sole and exclusive property of [Company Name]. The Contractor agrees to assign, and hereby assigns, all rights, title, and interest in the Work Product to [Company Name], including all copyright, patent, trademark, and other intellectual property rights.
- The Contractor agrees to execute any documents and take any actions reasonably necessary to perfect, protect, or enforce [Company Name]'s rights in the Work Product. The Contractor warrants that the Work Product is original, does not infringe upon the rights of any third

party, and has not been previously assigned, licensed, or otherwise transferred.
- [CONTRACTOR NAME] may showcase the completed Work Product in a personal portfolio, including websites, social media, or other self-promotional channels, provided that either (i) the project has been publicly launched, or (ii) [YOUR COMPANY NAME] provides written approval — whichever comes first.

Conditions:

- No confidential information may be shared, including but not limited to strategies, budgets, pricing, analytics, client contacts, or internal timelines. If requested, [CONTRACTOR NAME] must anonymize the Work Product by removing client names, logos, or other identifying information.

- All portfolio displays must clearly credit [YOUR COMPANY NAME] as the commissioning party (e.g., "Created for [YOUR COMPANY NAME]").

- [YOUR COMPANY NAME] may revoke permission at any time. Upon written notice, [CONTRACTOR NAME] must remove the Work Product from all portfolio channels within three (3) business days.

Termination

- Either party may terminate this Agreement with [e.g., 14 days] written notice.
- The Company may terminate immediately for cause, including violation of Company policies, breach of this Agreement, misconduct, or failure to perform duties.

Governing Law

This Agreement shall be governed by and construed under the laws of the State of [State]. Any disputes arising under this Agreement shall be resolved in the courts of [County/State].

Entire Agreement

This Agreement represents the entire understanding between the Parties and supersedes all prior negotiations, agreements, or communications. Modifications must be in writing and signed by both Parties.

IN WITNESS WHEREOF, the Parties have executed this Agreement as of the date first written above.

Company

Signature: _____

Name: _____

Title: _____

Date: _____

Contractor

Signature: _____

Name: _____

Date: _____

Optional Additions You Could Include:

- **Background Checks:** Contractors must provide a background check before onboarding.
- **Safety & Event Compliance:** Contractor agrees to follow all safety protocols at events.
- **Media Release:** Contractor grants the Company permission to use photos, videos, or recordings in which they appear.
- **Force Majeure:** Limits liability for delays caused by events outside the Contractor's control.

Sample Training Protocols

Participant Information

Name: _____

Role: ☐ Support Person ☐ Contractor

Event Name: _____

Date(s) of Event: _____

Trainer: _____

Training Date: _____

Purpose of This Training

This training ensures that all event support persons and contractors understand their role, expectations, and responsibilities. Our goal is to create safe, organized, and welcoming events where everyone knows what to do, who to report to, and how to support participants and the community.

Understanding Your Role

Check the areas you are responsible for:

- ☐ Setup and breakdown support
- ☐ Participant guidance and assistance
- ☐ Room monitoring and flow control
- ☐ Supply distribution or support
- ☐ Vendor or speaker support
- ☐ Observation and issue reporting

☐ General event support as assigned

In your own words, describe your role for this event:

_____

_____

_____

Chain of Command and Communication

Who do you report to?

Name: _____

How will you communicate during the event?

- ☐ In person
- ☐ Phone call
- ☐ Text message
- ☐ Group chat

If something goes wrong, who do you contact first?

_____

_____

Professional Conduct Expectations

Read and initial each statement.

- ☐ I will arrive on time and stay for my assigned shift. _____
- ☐ I will dress appropriately and wear any required credentials. _____
- ☐ I will be respectful to participants, staff, and vendors. _____
- ☐ I will not use drugs or alcohol before or during the event. _____

☐ I understand I represent the organization at all times. _____

Safety and Emergency Awareness

☐ I know where emergency exits are located.

☐ I know who to contact in case of an emergency.

☐ I understand how to report safety concerns immediately.

Emergency Contact Person: _____

One safety concern I should always watch for:

_____

_____

Participant Interaction and Support

When interacting with participants, I will:

☐ Be welcoming and approachable

☐ Provide clear and accurate information

☐ Ask for help if I am unsure of an answer

☐ Respect participant privacy and confidentiality

Example:

If a participant appears confused or frustrated, what should you do?

_____

_____

_____

Event Flow and Flexibility

Events do not always go exactly as planned. Support persons and contractors must remain flexible.

- ☐ I understand schedules may change.
- ☐ I understand tasks may shift during the event.
- ☐ I will remain calm and solution-focused.

What does "stay flexible" mean to you in this role?

Accountability and Problem Reporting

- ☐ If I notice an issue, I will report it immediately.
- ☐ I will not attempt to fix major problems without approval.
- ☐ I will document issues if asked.

Example issues you might need to report:

Confidentiality and Boundaries

- ☐ I understand not all information is meant to be shared publicly.
- ☐ I will not post photos or videos without approval.
- ☐ I will respect personal and organizational boundaries.

Acknowledgment and Agreement

I acknowledge that I have completed this training worksheet, understand my role, and agree to follow all expectations for this event.

Name (Printed): _____

Signature: _____

Date: _____

Trainer Signature: _____

Date: _____

Training Reminder

Support roles are the backbone of successful events. When you show up prepared, professional, and flexible, everything else flows.

Sample Invoice

[Your Company Name / Logo]
[Address]
[City, State ZIP]
[Phone] | [Email] | [Website]

Invoice Number: [001]
Invoice Date: [MM/DD/YYYY]
Due Date: [MM/DD/YYYY]

Bill To:
[Client Name / Company]
[Client Address]
[City, State ZIP]
[Client Email]

Description of Services / Products

Item / Service	Description	Qty / Hours	Unit Price	Total
[Service Name]	[Brief description]	[1 / X hrs]	[$XXX.XX]	[$XXX.XX]
[Service Name]	[Brief description]	[1 / X hrs]	[$XXX.XX]	[$XXX.XX]
Subtotal				[$XXX.XX]
Tax (X%)				[$XX.XX]
Total Due				[$XXX.XX]

Payment Instructions:

Please make payments via [Bank Transfer, PayPal, Stripe, etc.] to:

[Bank Account / Payment Link / Instructions]

Notes / Terms:

Payment is due within [X] days of the invoice date. Late payments may be subject to [X]% late fee.

Thank you for your business!

Sample Order Form

General Information

Organization Name: _____ Department/Project:_____

Requestor Name: _____ Date of Request: _____

Delivery Location: _____ Contact Email/Phone: _____

Order Details

Item No.	Item Description	Quantity	Unit Price	Total Cost	Priority Level (High/Med/Low)	Notes

Cost Summary	
Subtotal	
Tax (if applicable):	
Shipping & Handling:	
Grand Total:	

Approval Section

Supervisor Approval: _____ Supervisor Approval Date: _____

Procurement Approval: _____ Procurement Approval Date: _____

Marketing Guidelines for Programs, Workshops, and Initiatives

Purpose:

This guide provides best practices for designing, implementing, and measuring marketing efforts for programs. It helps ensure your messaging reaches the right audience, attracts diverse participants, and aligns with stakeholder requirements.

Design & Messaging

- Keep your materials visually appealing and clear.
- Ensure messaging communicates the purpose, value, and audience benefit.
- Use inclusive language to attract diverse audiences.
- Include branding for your organization and co-brand with partners as required.

Marketing Platforms & Methods

Platform/Method	Audience/Use Case	Benefits
Social Media (Instagram, Facebook, LinkedIn, TikTok)	Younger audiences, professional networks	Broad reach, engagement, shareable content
Event Platforms (Eventbrite, Meetup)	Event registration and RSVP tracking	Easy registration, automated reminders
Email/Text Messaging	Existing contacts, stakeholders	Personalized outreach, high engagement
Word of Mouth/ Community Leaders	Local residents and networks	Builds trust, leverages influence
Flyers/Posters (Community Centers, Grocery Stores)	Foot traffic in specific neighborhoods	Reaches non-digital audiences
Tagging Partners/ Vendors	Partner organizations and collaborators	Expands reach and strengthens partnerships

Co-Branding & Approvals

- Confirm all materials are approved by stakeholders before distribution.
- Ensure logos, fonts, and messaging align with partner branding guidelines.
- Set clear deadlines for feedback to avoid delays.

Measurement & Tracking

- Track marketing effectiveness using quantitative and qualitative methods:
    - Social media engagement (likes, shares, comments)
    - Event registrations and attendance
    - Click-through rates and inquiries
    - Community feedback or surveys
- Record which platforms or messages perform best to inform future campaigns.

Follow-Up & Adjustments

- Check in with clients or partners after campaigns to review results.
- Adjust messaging or channels if engagement is low.
- Document lessons learned for continuous improvement.

Branding Guide

[Your Organization] Branding Guide

Purpose: This guide provides standards for using the organization's visual and verbal identity to maintain consistency across all communications, marketing materials, and events. Consistent branding helps build trust, recognition, and professionalism.

Logo

- **Primary Logo:** Use the full-color logo on all official materials.
- **Secondary Logo / Icon:** Use simplified or monochrome versions for smaller spaces or digital icons.
- **Do Not:** Stretch, rotate, or alter the logo colors or proportions.

Colors

Color Name	Hex Code	Use Case
Primary Blue	#1A73E8	Main headers, logos, call-to-actions
Medium Gray	#6C6C6C	Text, subheaders, backgrounds
Accent Yellow	#FFC107	Highlights, buttons, key visuals

Typography

- **Primary Font:** Open Sans (for headings)
- **Secondary Font:** Roboto (for body text)
- **Guidelines:**
    - Heading sizes: H1 = 36px, H2 = 28px, H3 = 22px
    - Body text: 14–16px for readability
    - Avoid using more than two fonts in a single piece of content

Imagery & Photography

- Use high-quality images that reflect diversity and community engagement.
- Avoid stock images that appear generic or staged.
- Photos should be bright, natural, and relevant to program content.

Tone & Voice

- **Voice:** Professional, warm, and approachable
- **Tone:** Positive, empowering, and inclusive
- **Do Not:** Use jargon or language that excludes any group

Social Media Guidelines

- Profile photos should use the logo or a recognizable symbol.
- Cover images should align with event branding and color palette.
- Posts should be consistent with brand voice and tone.
- Always tag partners, co-brand when required, and maintain approval process for campaigns.

Co-Branding Standards

- Place partner logos in a secondary position behind your primary logo.
- Keep consistent spacing and sizing rules.
- Ensure colors and typography do not conflict.
- Obtain approval from all parties before publishing.

Templates & Materials

- **Documents:** Use official letterhead for proposals, contracts, and reports.
- **Slides:** Include logo in top-right corner, primary color as header, secondary color for text.
- **Flyers & Social Media Graphics:** Use consistent fonts, colors, and imagery aligned with the brand guide.

Contact for Branding Questions

- [Branding Lead Name]
- Email: [email@example.com]
- Phone: [XXX-XXX-XXXX]

This guide ensures everyone representing your organization does so consistently, professionally, and in a way that reinforces your mission and vision.

Guide for Holding a Planning Meeting With a CBO

1. Welcome and Purpose (5 minutes)
   - **Greet participants** warmly and thank them for joining.
   - **State the meeting's purpose**: To walk through the event planning process collaboratively and transparently, review the Memorandum of Understanding (MOU), and finalize logistics.
   - Share the **meeting agenda** on the screen or in print.

2. Review the MOU (10 minutes)
   - **Display the signed MOU** on the screen (or a draft if still under review).
   - Briefly go over key sections:
     - Scope of work
     - Roles and responsibilities
     - Budget terms
     - Deliverables and timelines
     - Reporting expectations (Evaluations)
   - Allow time for **questions or clarification**.

3. Present the Budget (10 minutes)
   - Open a prepared **Excel sheet** with the full CBO budget (e.g., **$XX,XXX**).
   - Clearly break down **budget categories**, such as:
     - Personnel
       - Staff: explain we can pay for two people at a rate of $XXX.XX each
       - Logistics Vendor: explain we can pay for the logistics team to move day of supplies
     - Supplies and materials
     - Food vendors/catering

- Venue costs
- Highlight the **in-kind donation $X, XXX** to the organization for supporting the event.
- Explain **allowable vs. unallowable costs**.

4. Walk Through the Planning Guide (15–20 minutes)
   - Share your **event planning guide live on screen**.
   - Walk through it section by section, discussing:
     - Timeline and major deadlines
     - Outreach and promotion strategies
     - Workshop format and content
     - Staffing needs and responsibilities
     - Materials and supplies checklist
     - Evaluation/feedback tools
   - Confirm action items and **assign roles/responsibilities**.

5. Design the Room Layout (10–15 minutes)
   - Open **PowerPoint** and use a slide to collaboratively design the event **room layout**:
     - Tables/chairs
     - Sign-in area
     - Food station
     - Breakout spaces
     - Accessibility considerations
   - Adjust the layout in real-time based on CBO input.

6. Confirm Next Steps & Meeting Frequency (5 minutes)
   - Review key action items and **who is responsible** for each.
   - Confirm the **frequency of future planning meetings** (e.g., weekly, biweekly).
   - Set the date and time for the **next check-in meeting**.

7. Close the Meeting (5 minutes)
    - Recap what was covered and **thank the CBO** for their partnership.
    - Ask if there are any **final questions or feedback**.
    - Share a copy of the budget, planning guide, and PowerPoint layout after the meeting.

Sample Media Release Form

Participant Name: _____

Date of Birth: _____

Event / Program Name: _____

Date(s) of Event / Program: _____

Grant of Permission

I hereby grant [Your Company], its representatives, employees, and agents the right to photograph, film, or record me (or my child/ward) during the above-listed event/program. I consent to the use of these photographs, videos, or audio recordings in any format for educational, promotional, marketing, or social media purposes.

Usage Rights

I understand that the media may be used in print, online, social media, or other digital media platforms. I waive any right to inspect or approve the finished product and acknowledge that I will not receive any compensation for the use of these materials.

Release of Liability

I release [Your Company] and all associated parties from any liability that may arise from the use of these media materials.

Voluntary Agreement

I acknowledge that I have read and understand this Media Release Form and voluntarily agree to its terms.

Signature (Participant / Parent or Guardian if under 18):

_____

Date: _____

Printed Name: _____

Sample Participant Liability Waiver & Assumption of Risk Form

Participant Name:

_____

Event / Program Name:

_____

Date of Birth:

_____

Date(s) of Event / Program:

_____

Acknowledgment of Risk

I acknowledge that participation in this program or event may involve inherent risks, including but not limited to: physical activity, exposure to weather, and other unforeseen risks. I voluntarily assume full responsibility for any risks, injuries, or damages that may occur during participation.

Health & Safety

I certify that I am in good health and capable of participating safely in this event/program. I agree to follow all safety rules and guidelines established by [Your Company].

Release of Liability

I release, waive, discharge, and hold harmless [Your Company], its staff, volunteers, and partners from any liability, claims, demands, or causes of action arising out of or relating to my participation in this event/program.

Emergency Medical Authorization

In the event of an emergency, I authorize the program staff to seek medical attention for me and agree to be responsible for any costs incurred.

Voluntary Agreement

I have read this waiver carefully, understand its contents, and sign it voluntarily.

Signature (Participant / Parent or Guardian if under 18):

_____ **Date:** _____

Printed Name: _____

Sample Sign-In Sheets

Participant ID	Name	Contact Information

Run of Show Template

Workshop Title

Title:	
Date & Location	
Target Audience	
Target # of Participants	
Objectives	
Incentives	
Evaluation	

Staff Members

Team	Staff		
	Staff/Volunteer	Contact Information	Day of Assignment
Logistics			
Registration & Evaluation			
Greeters			
Supplier (Food)			

Run of Show Table

Time	Task	Notes	Persons of Interest	Point of Contact
	Staff Arrival			
	Tables Setup			
	Vendor Arrival			
	Food Setup			
	Staff Placement			
	Brunch			
	Registration			
	Pre-Evaluation			
	Program Begin			
	Post-Evaluation			
	Meet the Vendors			
	Breakdown & Cleanup			

Room Layout Template

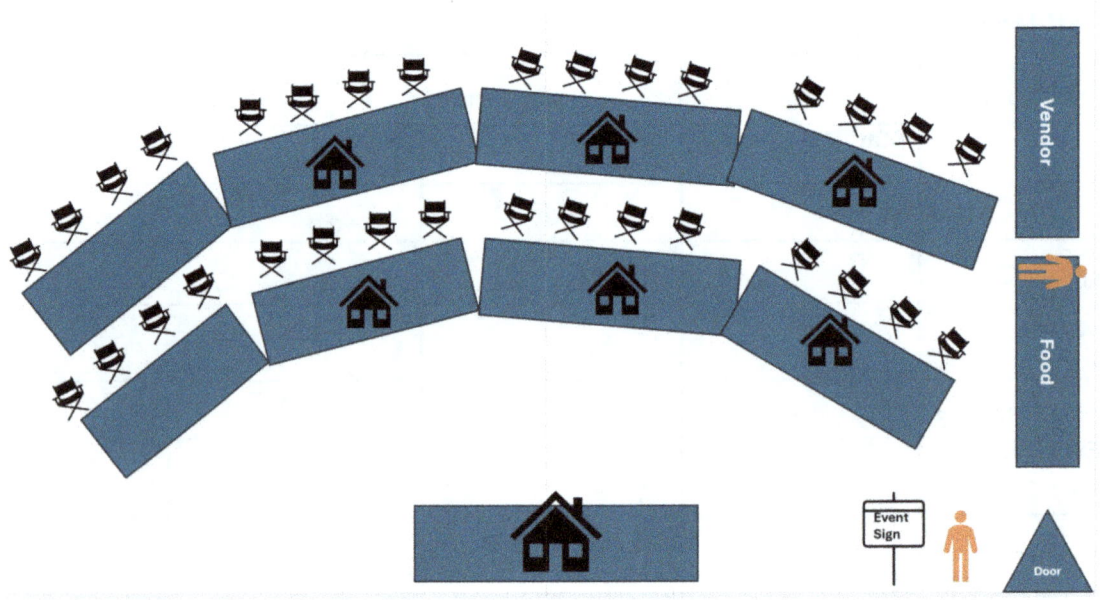

Community Program Budget Template

Program Name: [Insert Program Name]

Date(s): [Insert Date(s)]

Location: [Insert Location]

Prepared By: [Your Name]

Version: [Insert Version / Date]

Category	Item / Description	Unit Cost	Quantity	Subtotal	Notes
Personnel	Program Coordinator	$		$	Salary / stipend
	Facilitators / Trainers	$		$	Per session or day
	Support Staff / Volunteers	$		$	Stipends or hourly wages
	Guest Speakers	$		$	Honorariums or travel
Materials & Supplies	Workshop Materials	$		$	Handouts, worksheets, pens, markers
	Safety / Disaster Kits	$		$	Kits for participants
	Giveaways / Incentives	$		$	T-shirts, water bottles, etc.
	Office Supplies	$		$	Paper, folders, labels
Venue & Facilities	Rental Fee	$		$	Room, tables, chairs
	Audio/Visual Equipment	$		$	Microphones, projectors, screens
	Cleaning / Setup	$		$	Janitorial or setup fees
Food & Beverages	Catering / Meals	$		$	Breakfast, lunch, snacks
	Drinks & Water	$		$	Coffee, tea, water bottles
Transportation & Travel	Staff Travel	$		$	Mileage, rideshare, or vehicle rental
	Participant Travel Assistance	$		$	Bus vouchers or transportation stipends
Marketing & Communications	Flyers / Posters	$		$	Design & printing
	Social Media / Ads	$		$	Paid promotions
	Photography / Video	$		$	Event coverage
Contingency	Emergency Fund	$		$	5-10% of total budget for unexpected costs
Other Expenses	Insurance / Permits	$		$	Liability, event insurance
	Miscellaneous	$		$	Any additional expenses not listed
TOTAL				$	

Program Impact and Success Measures

Guidance: As the implementing partner, you will be expected to demonstrate impact across **four core areas**: reach, engagement, outcomes, and sustainability. Success will be measured using both **quantitative data and qualitative insights**.

1. Reach and Access

These measures assess whether the program is reaching the intended audience.

- **Number of Participants Served:** Track total attendance, repeat participation, and demographic breakdowns to ensure the program reaches the intended community.

- **Community Representation:** Measure participation from priority populations, including residents of impacted areas, frontline communities, or historically underserved groups.

- **Geographic Access:** Document where programming occurs and assess whether locations reduce transportation and access barriers.

2. Engagement and Participation Quality

These measures assess how participants interact with the program.

- **Attendance Retention Rate:** Measure how many participants complete the full program or attend multiple sessions.

- **Active Participation:** Track participation in discussions, activities, surveys, and hands-on components.

- **Stakeholder Involvement:** Document the number of community-based organizations, leaders, and local partners involved as co-creators rather than just attendees.

3. Learning and Behavioral Outcomes

These measures assess whether the program leads to meaningful change.

- **Pre and Post Knowledge Gains:** Use surveys to measure increases in knowledge, awareness, or understanding related to program goals.

- **Confidence and Self Efficacy:** Measure participants' reported confidence in applying what they learned.

- **Behavioral Intent or Action:** Track whether participants plan to or have taken action such as preparing emergency kits, attending follow up meetings, applying for resources, or sharing information with others.

4. Community Level Impact

These measures assess broader effects beyond individual participants.

- **Community Capacity Building:** Document new skills gained by local organizations, leaders, or volunteers.
- **Systems or Process Improvements:** Track changes such as new partnerships formed, policies influenced, or resources redirected as a result of the program.
- **Trust and Relationship Building:** Measure changes in trust between residents, organizations, and institutions through surveys or focus groups.

5. Program Satisfaction and Quality

These measures assess how the program is perceived.

- **Participant Satisfaction Scores:** Collect feedback on relevance, accessibility, facilitation quality, and usefulness.
- **Stakeholder Feedback:** Gather structured input from community partners and funders on collaboration effectiveness.
- **Cultural Responsiveness:** Assess whether participants felt respected, heard, and represented.

6. Sustainability and Longevity

These measures assess whether the impact lasts beyond the program period.

- **Tool and Resource Utilization:** Track continued use of toolkits, guides, or materials provided.
- **Local Ownership:** Measure the number of activities, programs, or initiatives continued by community partners after program completion.
- **Replication Potential:** Document whether the program model is adapted or requested by other communities.

7. Reporting and Accountability

These measures ensure transparency and accountability.

- **Timely Reporting:** Deliver clear, concise progress and final reports aligned with funder expectations.
- **Data Integrity:** Ensure accurate, ethical data collection and storage.

- **Lessons Learned and Recommendations:** Provide documented insights on what worked, what didn't, and how the program can be improved or scaled.

Definition of Success: From a funder perspective, this program will be considered successful if it:

- Reaches the intended community equitably
- Demonstrates measurable learning and behavioral outcomes
- Builds community capacity rather than dependency
- Creates partnerships that last beyond the funding period
- Provides clear, transparent reporting and actionable insights

Sample Partner Feedback Form

Thank you for partnering with us on this workshop. Your feedback helps us enhance the quality and impact of future events.

Organization Name:

1. **Was the budget provided for your responsibilities sufficient to meet the goals of your involvement?**
   ☐ Yes
   ☐ Somewhat
   ☐ No
   Please explain:

2. **Was the stipend for your organization or team members appropriate for the time and effort involved?**
   ☐ Yes
   ☐ Somewhat
   ☐ No
   Please explain:

3. **How would you rate the overall planning and implementation process (e.g., clarity of roles, deadlines, coordination)?**
   ☐ Excellent
   ☐ Good
   ☐ Fair
   ☐ Poor
   Comments:

4. **How would you rate the process for requesting, receiving, and managing supplies and materials?**
   ☐ Very efficient
   ☐ Efficient
   ☐ Neutral
   ☐ Inefficient
   ☐ Very inefficient

Comments: _____

5. How sufficient and effective were the planning meetings?
☐ Very effective and frequent
☐ Effective, but could be more frequent
☐ Neutral
☐ Not very effective
☐ Ineffective or infrequent
Comments: _____

6. Organization Name: _____

7. Your Role in the Event:
☐ Planning
☐ Logistics
☐ Outreach
☐ Facilitation
☐ Other: _____

8. Overall, how would you rate the success of the workshop(s)?
☐ Excellent
☐ Good
☐ Fair
☐ Poor

9. How effective was the communication between your organization and the planning team?
☐ Very effective
☐ Effective
☐ Neutral
☐ Ineffective
☐ Very ineffective

10. Were the goals and expectations for the event clearly communicated to you?
☐ Yes
☐ Somewhat
☐ No

11. How would you rate the participant engagement during the workshop(s)?
☐ Very high
☐ High

☐ Moderate
☐ Low
☐ Very low

12. What aspects of the workshop(s) worked well?
_____

13. What challenges or areas for improvement did you experience?
_____

14. Do you have suggestions for future workshop topics or formats?
_____

15. Would you be interested in partnering with us again?
☐ Yes
☐ Maybe
☐ No

16. Additional Comments:
_____

References

American Evaluation Association. (2018). *Guiding principles for evaluators.* https://www.eval.org

Anderson, L. W., & Krathwohl, D. R. (Eds.). (2001). *A taxonomy for learning, teaching, and assessing: A revision of Bloom's taxonomy of educational objectives.* Longman.

Babbie, E. R. (2021). The practice of social research (15th ed.). Cengage Learning.

Bloom, B. S., Engelhart, M. D., Furst, E. J., Hill, W. H., & Krathwohl, D. R. (1956). *Taxonomy of educational objectives: The classification of educational goals. Handbook I: Cognitive domain.* Longmans, Green.

Bryson, J. M. (2018). *Strategic planning for public and nonprofit organizations* (5th ed.). Jossey-Bass.

Centers for Disease Control and Prevention. (2011). *Introduction to program evaluation for public health programs: A self-study guide.* https://www.cdc.gov/evaluation/guide/index.htm

Dillman, D. A., Smyth, J. D., & Christian, L. M. (2014). Internet, phone, mail, and mixed-mode surveys: The tailored design method (4th ed.). John Wiley & Sons.

Dun & Bradstreet. (n.d.). *Get a D-U-N-S® number.* https://www.dnb.com/duns/get-a-duns.html

Enenkel, M., Papp, A., Veit, E., & Voigt, S. (2017, October). Top-down and bottom-up—A global approach to strengthen local disaster resilience. In 2017 IEEE global humanitarian technology conference (GHTC) (pp. 1-7). IEEE.

Financial Crimes Enforcement Network. (n.d.). *Beneficial ownership information (BOI) reporting*. U.S. Department of the Treasury. https://boiefiling.fincen.gov/

Gundlach, M., & McDonough, M. (2011, January). Top-down vs. bottom-up planning.

Hiles, A. (2011). Business continuity for dummies. John Wiley & Sons.

Internal Revenue Service. (n.d.). *Apply for an employer identification number (EIN) online*. https://www.irs.gov/businesses/small-businesses-self-employed/apply-for-an-employer-identification-number-ein-online

Israel, B. A., Eng, E., Schulz, A. J., & Parker, E. A. (2013). *Methods for community-based participatory research for health* (2nd ed.). Jossey-Bass.

Kirkpatrick, D. L., & Kirkpatrick, J. D. (2006). Evaluating training programs: The four levels (3rd ed.). Berrett-Koehler Publishers.

Knaflic, C. N. (2015). Storytelling with data: A data visualization guide for business professionals. John Wiley & Sons.

Nance, E. (2018). Making the Case for Community-Based Laboratories. Race, Place, and Environmental Justice After Hurricane Katrina: Struggles to Reclaim, Rebuild, and Revitalize New Orleans and the Gulf Coast, 97.

Patten, M. L., & Newhart, M. (2018). Understanding research methods: An overview of the essentials (10th ed.). Routledge.

Patton, M. Q. (2012). *Essentials of utilization-focused evaluation*. SAGE Publications.

Project Management Institute. (2021). *A guide to the project management body of knowledge (PMBOK® Guide)* (7th ed.). Project Management Institute.

Ries, A., & Ries, L. (2002). The 22 immutable laws of branding. HarperBusiness.

Saldaña, J. (2016). The coding manual for qualitative researchers (3rd ed.). SAGE Publications.

Stim, R., & Coffman, J. M. (2017). Business contracts for dummies (3rd ed.). John Wiley & Sons.

W.K. Kellogg Foundation. (2017). *Logic model development guide*. https://www.wkkf.org/resource-directory/resources/2004/01/logic-model-development-guide

United Way Worldwide. (2013). *Measuring program outcomes: A practical approach*. https://www.unitedway.org

United States Small Business Administration. (n.d.). *Choose a business structure*. https://www.sba.gov/business-guide/launch-your-business/choose-business-structure

---

About the Author

Dr. Joy Semien is a community educator, program manager, and capacity builder with over 15 years of experience designing, implementing, and evaluating community-centered programs. Her work sits at the intersection of education, disaster preparedness, environmental justice, and community engagement, with a focus on translating research and lived experience into practical tools communities can use immediately.

Raised in a fenceline community in Southeast Louisiana, Dr. Joy's lived experience shaped her commitment to equity, preparedness, and community-driven solutions. She has worked across grassroots organizations, nonprofits, schools, government agencies, and private-sector partners, gaining a deep understanding of how different systems operate—and how to navigate them effectively while centering community needs.

Dr. Joy holds a Bachelor of Science in Biology with a minor in Chemistry from Dillard University, a Master's degree in Urban Planning and Environmental Policy from Texas Southern University, and a PhD in Urban and Regional Sciences from Texas A&M University. Her academic training, combined with years of on-the-ground program management, informs her practical, no-nonsense approach to building programs that are both meaningful and measurable.

She is the founder of L.E.E.D. With Joy LLC, an education and consulting firm that supports organizations in instructional design, training, evaluation, and program development. She is also the founder of The K.A.P.S. Disaster Hub, which focuses on disaster preparedness, response, and recovery education for households, organizations, and communities.

Throughout her career, Dr. Joy has served as a speaker, trainer, and guest educator for universities, federal agencies, nonprofits, and community initiatives. She is known for her authenticity, clarity, and ability to break down complex concepts into engaging, interactive learning experiences.

This book reflects lessons learned, the hard way—through real projects, real challenges, and real growth. Dr. Joy's goal is simple: to help program managers, educators, and community leaders work smarter, protect their worth, and build programs that truly serve the people they are meant to support.

Other Books By Joy Semien

Community Development Books

Hazard Mitigation Training for Vulnerable Communities: A K.A.P.S. (Knowledge Attitude Preparedness and Skills) Approach

Disaster Workbooks (Available in Spanish)

A K.A.P.S. Guide to Preparing for Disasters: The Organization Edition

A K.A.P.S. Guide to Preparing for Disasters: The Family Edition

A K.A.P.S. Guide to Preparing for Disasters: Children's Edition

A K.A.P.S. Guide to Preparing for Disasters: College Edition

A K.A.P.S. Guide to Preparing for Disasters: Caregivers Edition

A K.A.P.S. Guide to Preparing for Disasters: Facilitators Guide

A K.A.P.S. Guide to Recover from Disasters

Children's Books

The Giant and The Fairy

Learn to Read with Dino & Friends

Learn to Write with Dino & Friends

Learn to Read with Dino & Friends

Learn to Count with Dino & Friends

A Dino & Friends Activity Book

Biblically Based Books

The Holy Ghost and Me: A 30-Day Devotion with The Creator, The Son, and The Holy Spirit

Declarations for My Future Husband

Praying For Oranges

Planning Books

My 6-Month Vision Planner

About L.E.E.D. With Joy LLC

Education • Engagement • Evaluation • Design

Who We Are

LEED With Joy LLC is an education and consulting firm that supports communities, nonprofits, schools, and businesses in designing, implementing, and evaluating programs that are inclusive, effective, and grounded in real-world community needs. Led by a community educator with over 15 years of experience, LEED With Joy bridges research, lived experience, and practical tools to help organizations move from ideas to impact. We specialize in translating complex topics—such as disaster preparedness, environmental justice, community engagement, and program management—into accessible, actionable learning experiences.

Our Approach: The LEED With Joy Method

Our work is guided by four core principles:

- **Listen** using both lived experience and data
- **Engage** by co-creating with communities and stakeholders
- **Empower** through education through interactive, culturally responsive learning
- **Drive** Change by designing programs, tools, and evaluations that lead to measurable outcomes. This approach ensures programs are not only well-designed but trusted, relevant, and sustainable.

Our Services

Instructional Design & Curriculum Development

- K–12, college, and adult learning curricula
- Interactive workshops, trainings, and toolkits
- Instructor guides, participant workbooks, and learning assessments

Workshops, Trainings & Facilitation

- Community education workshops
- Professional development and capacity-building training
- Youth, family, and caregiver-focused learning experiences
- In-person, virtual, and hybrid delivery

Program Planning & Management Support

- Program design and implementation support
- Community engagement strategies
- Stakeholder coordination and facilitation
- Event and initiative planning

Monitoring, Evaluation & Learning (MEL)

- Program evaluation frameworks
- Surveys, focus groups, and qualitative analysis
- Funder-ready reports and impact summaries

Community & Organizational Capacity Building

- Support for grassroots and community-based organizations
- Guidance on operational setup and documentation
- Templates, tools, and systems for sustainable growth

Who We Serve

- Community-based organizations and nonprofits
- Schools, colleges, and universities
- Foundations and funders
- Local governments and agencies
- Small businesses and community coalitions

Our Commitment

LEED With Joy is committed to equity-centered practice, authentic community engagement, and practical solutions. We believe strong programs are built with communities—not just for them—and that education should always lead to empowerment, readiness, and action.

www.ingramcontent.com/pod-product-compliance
Lightning Source LLC
Chambersburg PA
CBHW080731230426
43665CB00020B/2702